Have You Ever Wondered...

- Why they hold fire drills in the rain?
- Why kids stand on line for yucky cafeteria food?
- Why schools always have a garbled P.A. system?
- Why some kids go to class *early*?
- Why the teacher *always* calls on you when you don't know the answers and *never* calls on you when you do?

You're not alone... every kid who has ever walked a school corridor has had the same questions. In *Stuff Your Guidance Counselor Never Told You*, J. Brent Bill explores the questions that occupy your mind when you're supposed to be working through geometric proofs... writing English compositions... or responding to the question, *¿Como se llama?*

Writing under the guise of Dr. Rufus Leaking, the author shows how the sometimes amusing, sometimes annoying situations you deal with in high school are precursors to those you'll encounter after graduation. Brent Bill intersperses his humorous musings with some down-to-earth counsel that's just as pertinent (sometimes even more) as what you're learning in school. *Stuff Your Guidance Counselor Never Told You* will help you stay on the right track in high school — and beyond.

Stuff Your Guidance Counselor
NEVER TOLD YOU

BY J. Brent Bill

Rock and Roll
Stay Tuned
Lunch Is My Favorite Subject
Cruisin' and Choosin'
Stuff Your Guidance Counselor Never Told You

Stuff Your Guidance Counselor
NEVER TOLD YOU

J. BRENT BILL

Power Books

Fleming H. Revell Company
Old Tappan, New Jersey

Library of Congress Cataloging-in-Publication Data

Bill, J. Brent.
　Stuff your guidance counselor never told you / J. Brent Bill.
　　p.　cm.
　Summary: Presents humorous answers to questions about high school life from new students and discusses how to cope by relying on one's Christian faith.
　ISBN 0-8007-5364-X
　1. High school students—Conduct of life. 2. Teenagers—Conduct of life. 3. High school students—Religious life. 4. Teenagers—Religious life. 5. Christian life. [1. Conduct of life.
2. Christian life. 3. High schools. 4. Schools. 5. Questions and answers.] I. Title.
BJ1661.B483　1990
248.8'3—dc20　　　　　　　　　　　　　　　　　　90-36758
　　　　　　　　　　　　　　　　　　　　　　　　　　　CIP
　　　　　　　　　　　　　　　　　　　　　　　　　　　AC

Jacket and interior illustrations by Rob Suggs.

All rights reserved. No part of this publication may be reproduced, stored in a retrieval system, or transmitted in any form or by any means—electronic, mechanical, photocopy, recording, or any other—except for brief quotations in printed reviews, without the prior permission of the publisher.

Copyright © 1990 by J. Brent Bill
Published by the Fleming H. Revell Company
Old Tappan, New Jersey 07675
Printed in the United States of America

TO
JoAnn Bill and Eloise Bill
(also known as Mom and Grandma),
who always stood ready to offer
both guidance and counsel—
some of which I took

Stuff Your Guidance Counselor
NEVER TOLD YOU

1

Where do you go to get help? That's a question every high school student asks. There's a lot of stuff going on in high school that didn't happen in junior high or middle school. More choice in classes. Bigger buildings. New teachers. Everyone needs some help. So where do you go to get help? Many answers may come to mind. Parents. Friends. Guidance counselors. These all seem like good answers. They all have one thing in common. They are all wrong.

   I know this goes against all your training, as well as vast experience in taking tests, which are made up mostly of questions. Since "Where do you go to get help?" is a question, you think you can figure this out. But can you? Generally while taking a test, particularly an objective one (which is a subject we'll get to later), one should always go with one's primary instinct. In studentese that means go with the first thing that pops into your head. This will usually work out if the question is one like the following:

   What is the capital of Hungary?

   You most likely will immediately think, *Budapest,* and be right. You're sure you're right, until you begin to think about it. And the more you think about it the less sure you become. Maybe it's Sofia. Or Sylvia. Or Crest toothpaste. The longer you think, the more muddled you become. And while trying to divine the correct answer for the first question on the test—"It's Stalingrad—except that's called Volgograd now. Nope, it's Peoria. Wait a minute, I'll bet it's . . ."—you've wasted two whole periods. While you've been thinking, the world has gone on. They've even held another class or two in the room while you've been so immersed in the answer you've probably forgotten the question. And the other forty-three questions never even got read. Worst of all, you missed the only one you did read.

So what's my point? Well, put simply, what works in objective tests does not work in real life. Here you do need to think about the answer. It could make all the difference.

Let's look at the responses above. "Responses to what?" you ask. Responses to the original question, which the above illustration concerning the truism of using the first answer that pops into your brain has caused you to forget. "Where do you go for help?"

The answers were—parents, friends, and guidance counselors.

Let's eliminate the easiest one first—friends. Can you take this answer seriously? What do your friends know that you don't know? They're stuck with the same questions that you have. Do you really think they know anything? How smart can they be? They're your friends, after all. You don't hang around with them because they are rocket scientists or brain surgeons (even if Wayne did pretend to be one while dissecting that frog in biology class). No. The reason you hang around with them is that they aren't smart. They are fun. They're sensitive. They like you. You like them. They may get good grades, but that's not why you hang around them. Maybe it's why you *should*, but it's not why you do.

So you need to cross friends off the list. Yes, you may go to them for help with the hard questions like who has the best pizza in town. Academic counseling is something else. After all, are you really going to take advice from someone you've known all your life and have always called "Pookie"?

Next come parents. They're always saying things like, "If you need help, call me." Which is nice. It's not helpful, but it is nice. It's what they learned to say at Parents School. Not that you *would* call them. These are, after all, the same folks who have lied to you all your life. First they tell you there's a person named Santa Claus. You build your hopes around this man in a red suit who slides down chimneys with toys for good little girls and boys. You try your best to behave. This at an age when sitting still for more than 15 seconds is an impossibility. You try for years and years to meet the ideal that old Saint Nick has for children. You torment yourself at night by lying awake and trying to remember if you did anything *naughty*. You don't worry about the nice, because you're pretty sure you didn't do anything like that. You pray you didn't do anything to cancel out Christmas entirely. He is coming, isn't he?

Terror reigns in children's bedrooms from Thanksgiving till 5:00 A.M. Christmas morning.

After all that, they tell you there's no such thing as Santa. "Why, honey, Santa is just your dad all dressed up like that. We buy all your presents ourselves—at K mart."

Ohmigosh. What a shock. How could it be any worse? They buy them at K mart?! You could just die.

But you don't. You call up vast reserves of strength from deep within your six-year-old body. Plus, there's still the Easter Bunny. Sure, when you think about it, it would be awfully hard for a guy as fat as Santa to make it all around the world. You never were too sure about eight tiny flying reindeer. Your parents never could satisfactorily answer your "But we don't have a chimney on the house here in Death Valley; how will he get in?" question. You were pretty silly to be taken in by that. Thank heavens the Easter Bunny still—hey, wait a minute. How does he hop all around the world? You've never seen a bunny carry anything, let alone wear a vest and make chocolate. They've lied to you again.

And after that, you find out that they've lied to you about other things. Things like—

> It really doesn't hurt them more than it hurts you.
> You don't have to "listen and listen good 'cause" they're "only going to tell you once."
> You'll get to hear it again. And again. And again.

They've lied about lots of things, like the stork bringing you or their finding you under a rock. (Although there are times they'd like to believe the last one—it would absolve them of any responsibility.)

Nope, don't go to your parents for help. Next thing you know, they'll be telling you stuff like, "These are the best years of your life," and other nonsense.

Finally, there are the guidance counselors. I'll give you two reasons not to trust them:

1. They are adults. "What's that got to do with it?" you ask. Well, the fact is, they are flawed by the mere fact that they are adults. Adults, you see, are unable to tell teenagers the truth. It's a genetic character flaw. As soon as people become adults, they lie to kids. It's not that they want to. They really aren't aware they are lying. They are convinced they are telling the truth. But they aren't. They just can't. Try as they might, the truth just won't come out.

2. Has a guidance counselor ever told you the stuff you really need to know anyhow? No. That's because they deal in broad generalities. Things like "What is life?" "How do I get into a good college?" and "How do I get started on the proper career path?" Those are nice, but you need specifics. You want things like "Where's the closest bathroom?" "When's my lunch period?" and "Is Mr. Cole's hair naturally purple?" That's right, the hard questions.

Now that I've shown you why your answers are wrong, I want to give you the right one. The questions in this book are the kinds of questions you would ask. As a matter of fact, many of you from around the country did ask them. They are teenager-asked questions. The answers come from noted child psychologist (he got his Ph.D. when he was five), Dr. Rufus Leaking. He is a leading authority on the kinds of questions you ask. He gives the answers you need and can rely on. You can trust him for three reasons:

1. He is not your friend. As a matter of fact, I'm not even sure he would like you if he met you.

2. He is not a guidance counselor. I'm not sure what he is, but it's not a guidance counselor. Kids never come to him for advice about career paths, good colleges, or the meaning of life.

3. He is not an adult. Weren't you paying attention when I told you he was a *child* psychologist?

So sit back and see if this book doesn't answer your deepest questions. If not, well, then I guess you or your folks are out about $5.95.

2

DEAR DR. LEAKING:

WHY DO THEY HOLD FIRE DRILLS IN THE RAIN?

GREG FROM GAS CITY, INDIANA

Dear Greg:
   This has got to be one of the questions I am asked most often. That's why it's in this book. I mean I wouldn't want to answer a question that nobody else ever asked, now, would I? It wouldn't be fair to all of the readers. As I said, this is a common question. Which is why it was chosen to be the lead question in this soon-to-be best-seller. But before I answer this question we need to set the scene. Close your eyes and try to imagine the following:
   You've just gotten seated comfortably, as if there is any such thing as being comfortable in a school chair. It makes you wonder where they get those chairs, doesn't it? Everyone knows, mostly from experience, that there is no way you can get comfortable in one of them. Unless you are a contortionist or double-jointed or both. That's because the people who design school furniture were

Stuff Your Guidance Counselor

really born about 400 years too late. That's right, they should have been alive in 1590 and working in some mad emperor's torture chamber. It's obvious that they've studied for the job. After all, they have taken all the finer features of the rack, the Iron Maiden (no, not the rock group), and other assorted pieces from ancient history and Vincent Price movies and sold them to your school board in the guise of student furniture. But that's another story—or chapter.

The subject at hand is fire drills. So back to our imagining. You're as comfortable as you're going to get in school. Mr. Shaffer is up there lecturing away on the ramifications of intergalactic molecular matter as it interrelates to frog saliva, you've just had a nice lunch in the cafeteria (this is pretending, remember?), and it's raining so hard that you just saw a fellow coming out of biology class with two of every kind of experiment following him. You are ready to settle in for a nap. That's when it happens. The fire bell rings. You now have 4.3 seconds to clear the building along with the rest of the students. And you do. You even set a new record—4.1 seconds. This is not hard if you are attending a school that has a student body of 27. It's not even hard if you have 2,700 in the student body. After all, it's not real difficult to get students out of a school building. The hard part is getting them in. And keeping them in.

So when the bell rings, there is a mad rush for the door. Who knows, perhaps you got lucky and the building really is on fire. Maybe Jack Rowley, that little pyromaniac, finally got the trash can in the boys' room ablaze. Even now the entire Mullenville Fire Department may be careening recklessly through the city streets, narrowly avoiding blue-haired little old ladies walking dogs that look like oversized rats. All in a valiant, but futile, bid to save Mullenville High. But alas, the only smoke that can be seen is that rising from the top of Mr. Pierson's bald head as the cold rain hits it and turns to steam.

It's a fire drill. Not a real fire. No cause for hope. Just a drill.

Nobody complains at first. At least you're not sitting there listening to Mr. Shaffer drone on and on about quarks or quirks or kooks. But after you've been outside awhile, watching your Lee's become instantly "storm-washed" and are soaked to the bone, it's no fun. You begin to wonder why you're still there. After all, it's a just a drill. You've done what you were asked to do. Everyone cleared the building in record time. If you can get out in 4.1 seconds, why does it take 4.1 hours to get back in?

If you are confused, it's because you don't understand the purpose of school. You are under the impression that you are there to learn. That is partly true. You *are* there to learn. But you are under the delusion that learning is to take place in the classroom. That is false. Incorrect. Wrong-o.

Teachers know as well as you do that you won't learn anything in class. Unless it's by mistake. And so they go out of their way to provide you with a chance to learn. They send you outside, in the rain, or in minus 20–degree weather to teach you something. It works. You learn, not just something, but a lot of things. One thing you learn is that school fire drills are a lot like life. In fire drills, as in life, you hurry up and wait. You run out of the building at light speed and then you stand around. There's a lot of that in life when you're a kid. There's even more of it when you get to be an adult.

When you get older you'll hurry down to the Department of Motor Vehicles to get your license plate—and stand in line six hours with others who hurried down to the same place for the same reason. You'll hurry to get your taxes done by January 15 and wait until May 30 to receive your $4.50 refund (which is all the IRS gives you after checking your math). To hurry up and then wait is one of the things that fire drills in the rain are about. It's philosophy class without Socrates and Plato. (No those aren't two of the Teenage Mutant Ninja Turtles.)

Fire drills in the rain also teach you practical things—like how long it will take a person to freeze to death in minus-20 weather. This is something everyone should know.

Another thing fire drills in the rain teach you is that things will happen at a time you really don't want them to. Who would complain about a fire drill on a day that is sunny and 85 degrees? No one. You'd love to be out there for a few hours, chatting with your friends and catching some rays. But life isn't like that. Things happen to you when you really don't want them to. And there's nothing you can do about it, because just like the fire drill bell, they are controlled by unseen forces. Forces over which you have no control.

So, fire drills will be held when it's nasty and gross and never when it's pleasant or pleasurable because you are not there to have fun—you're there to learn.

Fire drills in the rain can teach us about life with God, too. Not that God has the mentality of teachers and principals. No, He's much nicer than that. But the fact is that what the teachers and principals want you to learn is true—things will happen to you when you don't want them to. God wants you to learn that, too. I don't believe God teaches you by sending bad things your way when you aren't ready for them. God is not the kind of person who has your parents get a divorce or makes your best friend die just to teach you something. Those kinds of things just happen. They are a part of life on this planet. That doesn't make them fun or easy or desirable. It's just reality.

But, if you will walk close to God, you can learn things about life when the awful things happen. You must stand quietly while life rains down on you, though, because it's when we're silent in the midst of misery that we can hear God speaking most clearly to us. Sometimes we need to shut up long enough to hear God talking. He very rarely shouts. More often, God's voice comes in a whisper. Softly. Like an easy spring rain falling upon us.

Fire drills may never be fun. And they are almost always in unpleasant weather. The next time you're standing there getting soaked, practice listening to God. The sound you hear may be His voice with some good news for you, about your life, your future, and the love He has for you.

Or it could be rain running down into your middle ear. See if you can learn to tell the difference.

3

DEAR DR. LEAKING:

THE CAFETERIA FOOD HERE IS AWFUL. WHY DO KIDS KEEP STANDING IN LINE FOR IT?

MARILYN IN MOOSIC, PENNSYLVANIA

Dear Marilyn:

On the surface, yours seems to be a pretty good question. It is true that cafeteria food is awful. This is not disputed by anyone, except the school administration. That's only because they are required by law to say that the food in the cafeteria is "nutritious, healthful, and good tasting" (*Rules Governing School Administrators,* chapter 13, "Lying to the Students About Food"). If you want to know why the food is so bad, read the definitive book—*Lunch Is My Favorite Subject,* also published by Revell. Besides the reasons enumerated in that tome, there is another reason. That is that in 47 of the 50 or so states in the United States, it is a law that school food

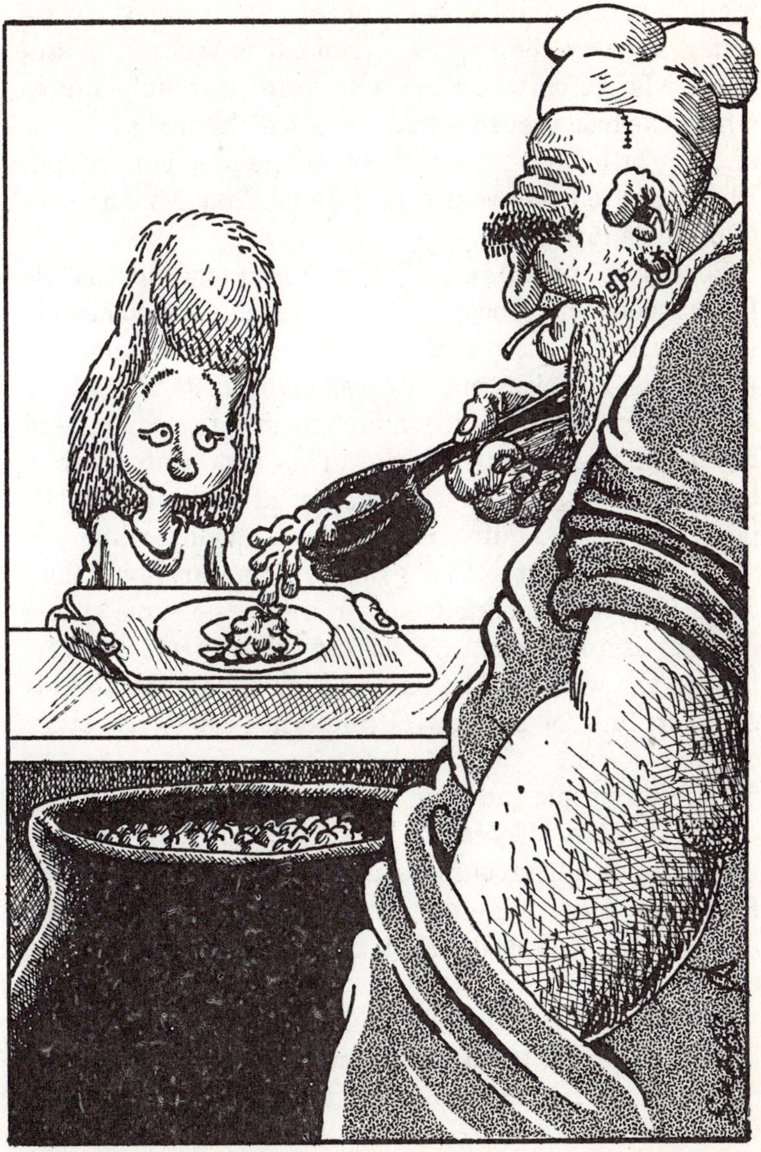

cannot be good. The main concept behind this is that many current high school students will attend private colleges where the food is terrible. The rest of the students who go on to college will go to state universities where the food is even worse. State legislators have mandated poor food as part of their college prep curriculum. They want to lower your expectations. And avoid breach-of-promise law suits.

So why do students stand in line to eat terrible food? At first it seems mind-boggling. Unbelievable. Stretches the imagination. Causes brain damage even to contemplate it. This is, however, one of those many instances where something seems too incomprehensible to comprehend but is in fact simply simple. (This last sentence was brought to you by the Department of Redundancy Department.) If you quit trying to think about it while you are thinking about it, the answer will appear. It will float down into your consciousness in much the same subtle manner as an irate teacher asking you why you are staring out the window. The answer is obvious. Why *do* kids stand in line for that awful cafeteria food? What other choice is there?

Let's face some sad facts here.

Sad Fact #1: There are very few school cafeterias in possession of a food court featuring a McDonald's, Rax, or Pizza Hut. You can't order something you like from your favorite fast-food feeding establishment. It's simply not available.

Sad Fact #2: Only nerds carry brown-bag lunches. I know, because a lot of my friends carried them (brown bags, not nerds), and sad to say my influence over them was so weak that many of them never made the transition from teenage mutant zit-faced nerds to the exalted state of cool where folks like you and I always reside. The only thing sadder than teenage mutant zit-faced nerds carrying brown-bag lunches are teenage mutant zit-faced nerds carrying Teenage Mutant Ninja Turtle lunch boxes. 'Nuff said.

Sad Fact #4 (#3 was so sad, I just couldn't bear to write about it): The main reason kids stand in line for stuff that the chimps on Monkey Island at the Columbus Zoo wouldn't eat is that, unlike the chimps on Monkey Island, they have nothing else to eat. If the chimps don't like the chow at the zoo, they just go sit back on the island. Pretty soon some visitor comes along, ignores the "Do Not Feed the Chimps" sign, and throws them peanuts, popcorn, parts of hot dogs, or their little sister. Voilà! (that's French for "Wow"). They have something to eat.

Now quick. Think back. When was the last time a visitor to your school threw something at your mouth—other than a left hook?

Sad Fact #5: Though the chimps have a choice and students do not, students have something over the chimps. Students have a higher IQ. It may not be a lot higher, but it is higher. And the kids in line, being of superior intelligence, with brain wave patterns somewhat higher than a slug, know that a little bit of rotten food goes a long way in a really good food fight.

No one wants to be caught in the cafeteria empty-handed and miss the opportunity to fling fettuccine or dodge donuts. And miss the chance to get expelled with the rest of the junior class? No thank you.

Sad Fact #6: "Hope springs eternal in the human breast." I didn't make that up. Some famous literary type

Stuff Your Guidance Counselor

did. A long, long time ago. In spite of that, it's still true. People keep hoping for something better. There's always the chance, remote though it may be, that someone in the cafeteria will goof up and serve something that tastes delicious. I mean really good. Sure, it would be a mistake of monumental proportions, but if one of the cooks was new and didn't know she was breaking *Wyoming State Code #391.b, Paragraph d:* "No edible food shall be served on school premises within the geographical boundaries of the contiguous borders of the great state of Wyoming..." and so on, then something really good might come along.

That's not to say you should expect it every day. But occasionally in the midst of the mundane and expected, something extraordinary happens.

The life of faith can be like that, too. Let's face it, much of life is pretty ordinary. Like cafeteria food can be. At other times life is just crummy, stinky, and generally worthless, like cafeteria food is most of the time. And every so often there are people who find that waiting in line with all the tedium and boredom and rotten stuff just a bit too much. So they step out of line. Permanently. I know they do; my best friend in high school did. Greg was convinced that life was a lot like standing in the cafeteria line—mostly bad, bad, bad. So he got a gun and took himself out of line. For good.

Sad Fact #7: Greg has missed a lot. Sure he's avoided the rotten and crummy and boring. But he's also missed the fun and excitement that life can bring. He never got to graduate from college. He never got to fall head over heels in love. He never even got to do something as simple as order a pizza from Domino's because there weren't any Domino's when he took himself out of the line.

Life is like being in the school cafeteria line. A lot of surprises come along in life. You meet special friends. You find a neat job. You fall in love with someone special. Good things happen when you least expect them. But sometimes you have to keep standing in line until they happen. You have to hang in there.

That's part of the reason for hanging in there. You don't want to miss the good things God can bring your way. And God does have plenty of fantastically good surprises in store for you. He really does. I know He's surprised me with more good things than I ever could have imagined when I was 16. And even though I'm old (probably almost dead on your scale), I'm staying in line. I'll put up with the crummy and boring, because pretty soon something great is going to be served up in this cafeteria.

Wanna grab a tray and join me?

4

DEAR DR. LEAKING:

WHY ARE MY CLASSES SO FAR APART WHEN I ONLY HAVE THREE MINUTES TO TRAVEL BETWEEN THEM?

LISA FROM LANDER, WYOMING

Dear Lisa:

There is a good reason it seems your classes are so far away when you only have three minutes to get from one to the other. It's because they are.

Scheduling classes is a science. Those who want to grow up to be schedulers have to spend years in preparation. But more about their training later. What they hope to achieve is the following—to make you travel as far as possible in as little time as possible. If it could be arranged, your schedule would be set so that you would have to travel an average of 6.5 miles between class periods. Part of learning the science of putting together class schedules is training oneself to accomplish this. If the scheduler could, he or she would put you in classes in different time zones. One right after the other.

The other part of the science of scheduling is making sure you don't get any of the classes you preregistered for last spring. But that's another question that no one has asked yet.

Yes, Lisa, class scheduling is a sophisticated twentieth-century science, filled with mathematical equations that would baffle an Einstein, Fermi, or even the Count from "Sesame Street."

It wasn't always this way. Class scheduling wasn't always a science. It used to be an art form taught only in teachers' colleges. It was an art form because it used to be done manually. (That's English for "by hand.") Back in the olden days (the sixties and earlier), schedules were actually put together by people who spent their hours and days thinking of ways to screw up yours. They met in rooms with map-covered walls and tables overflowing with blueprints of the school, and they had to use crude instruments like slide rules and watches with hands instead of digital readouts. They had to use these primitive things and put confusing schedules all together themselves. And they ended up doing very well. Even in the olden days, kids used to run to class, futilely trying to find their seats before the tardy bell rang. Every now and then, though, someone would slip up. A simple human error would occur and a student would find himself with classes in adjacent classrooms. No more. Thanks to modern technology such mistakes have been eliminated. The reign of student bewilderment marches on.

Yes, today, much in the same way that the only people making "authentic" American Indian pottery have

Stuff Your Guidance Counselor

names like Rikki, Tikki, or Tavi and live in the Far East, the only people making class schedules aren't people. They are computers. As IBM and its mighty microchips have changed the rest of the world, they have changed school, too. Though, as usual, the change took longer. Now, in place of gymnasiums reeking of the sweat of the human brow (and armpits) in the hot, humid days of summer and overflowing with charts, maps, slide rules, and wet teachers cackling madly at what they've done to you, a nice man in a white coat merely punches your name into his "Insaniac" computer and lets it work you over. All the possible permutations and perversions of your schedule appear on his video screen. All within the space of 1.3 nanoseconds, with the worst one at the top. What once took months, and began five minutes or less after you left the school building for summer vacation, now takes only an afternoon. In less time than it takes you to get a really good burn in the summer sun, havoc has been wreaked upon your scholastic schedule. You are doomed to wander for miles in minutes.

That's one reason why your classes are so far apart. That's the technical reason. That's the mechanical reason. That's how it happens. But, Lisa, there is a deeper question. It is also known as the *Philosophical Question*. And that question is, "Why?" Why do they want to do this to you in the first—or even, last—place? And the philosophical answer to the philosophical question is that someone once did it to them.

Though it is hard to believe, these decrepit, hunched-over, arthritic old people were once vital, fun-loving teenagers. Yes it was bizillions of years ago, but it is a fact. They were once young and full of hopes and dreams. They were happy and carefree. Then maniacal malfeasants known as principals set up schedules that made them travel from one end of the school to the other between classes.

For some of them this wasn't too hard because they went to one-room schools. But most of them went to bigger schools. Maybe even the same schools that you are attending now. And it meant that they were doomed to travel miles and miles to class. While this was happening to them, do you think they took an oath that if they were ever in the position of making out schedules they would get you like they had been got? Do you think they swore to work future generations over like they had been worked over? No! Far from it. Instead they solemnly swore the following sacred oath:

> "If I ever get a chance to make out a schedule I'll put the kids in classes right next to each other and give them twenty minutes in between so they can go to the bathroom or get a snack and arrive fresh and rested."

What happened, you ask, to this sacred oath, this holy vow?

They forgot it.

They didn't do it on purpose. It wasn't intentional. No, they forgot because they became adults. It is a little-known, but well-proven, fact that as soon as you become an adult you are afflicted with a terrible disease that affects the part of the brain where you store all the vows you vowed as a kid. These vows include, but are not limited to, the following:

"When I grow up I'll never treat my kids like that."

and

"No son of mine is going to have to eat spinach if he doesn't want to."

and

"When I have kids, I'll let them have ice cream and soda pop for breakfast if they want."

Everything they swore they'd never do, they do. Something awful has happened—they've turned into their parents. That's right, they say the same things their parents said. They do the same things their parents did. And they are not even aware of it. And the really scary thing is that the same thing is going to happen to *YOU!*

That's one thing that life teaches us. No matter how many times we say, "Well, I won't do . . ." we end up doing. . . . It's because it is what we learned. We have seen it so many times, it has become second nature. We think that's how kids are raised, how clothes are washed, how napkins are folded, and how school schedules are made.

We humans tend to be creatures of habit. We do things semiconsciously if we are conscious at all. To do something different takes effort.

That's true in our faith life, too. Sometimes we see someone who seems to have it more together in the faith area than we do. We know they read the Bible a lot and really know what it says. They pray more often than we do. As a result they seem to be calmer and more self-assured. They act like they know more about who God is and what it means to be a follower of Jesus than we do. And we would like to be like them. So, we think, we'll do what they do.

We'll read the Bible more often and say more prayers. We mean it. That's what we want to do. But we don't. We just don't. Mostly because it is easier not to.

To change, to really change, means we have to think a lot. We have to act a lot, too, because just thinking about changing doesn't change anything. So if you want to make a change in your faith life, quit thinking about it and start doing it.

You can even start small. Begin by reading your Bible for five minutes every day. Or starting each meal, even the ones in the school cafeteria, with a prayer. Come to think of it, the ones in the school cafeteria need the most prayer.

You may be starting small, but you will, at least, be starting. Things like reading and praying will become habits. Good habits. And pretty soon you will start changing. All because you did something about it.

Well, I hope I've answered your question, Lisa. But if you've been reading this between classes I've got some bad news for you. You still have 6.3 miles to go—and only 30 seconds left.

5

DEAR DR. LEAKING:

WHAT I WANT TO KNOW IS HOW COME ALL THE BIG GUYS ARE ON THE ONE TEAM IN GYM CLASS AND ALL THE SMALL ONES ARE ON THE OTHER?

MIKEY IN MILACA, MINNESOTA

Dear Mikey:

Yours is not a new question. As a matter of fact, it's one of the oldest questions around and dates back to Old Testament times. Our family history records that my ancestor, Rabbi Leaking, was approached with this same question by a young man named David who was getting ready for a gym class with some guys from Gath. But more about that later.

To begin, you need to remember why you are at school. No, it is not to kill time until you're 18, although some folks do seem to take that approach. Think back to the

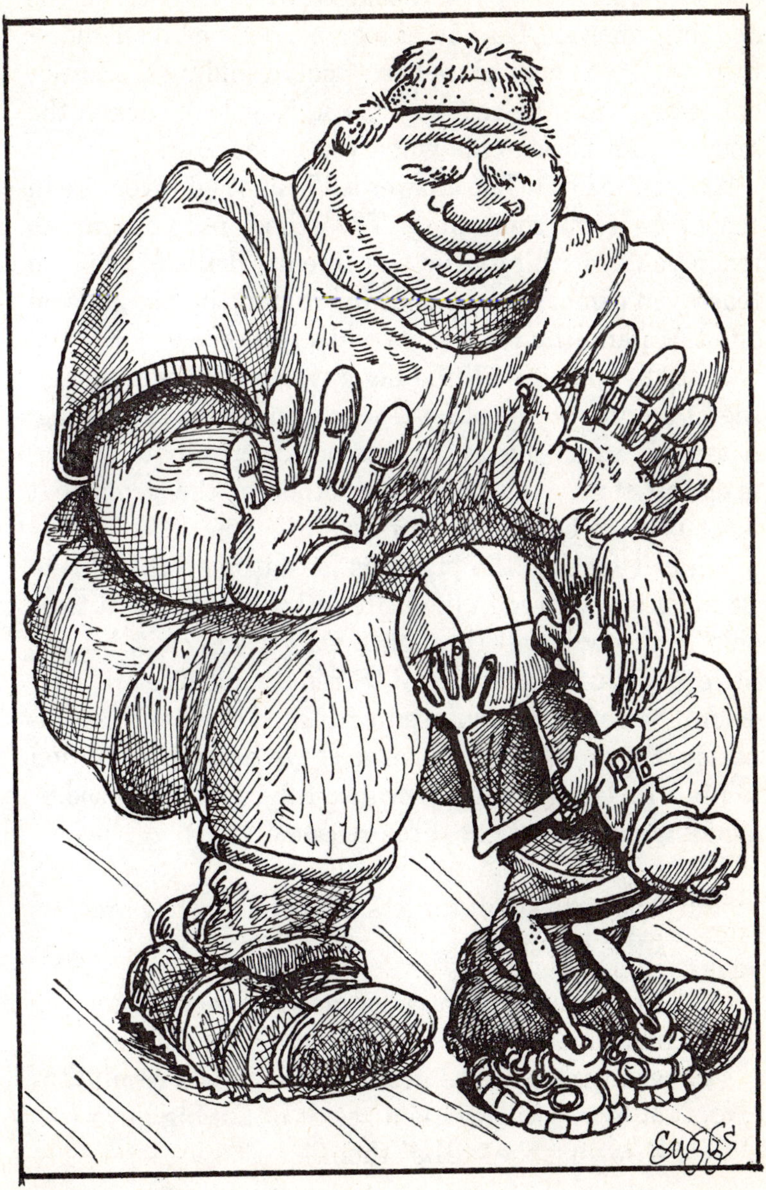

opening question of this book. Now think back to the opening answer. Do you remember any of it? I didn't think so. Mark your place here—not by folding the corner of the page down! Use a bookmark. Now look back at the answer. Get back to me when you've found it.

Ah, you're back. The answer is? That's right, you are in school to learn something. The school people want to teach you something. And just like fire drills in the rain teach you something, so does having all the big guys on one team and the little guys on the other.

Actually, putting all the big guys on one team and all the little guys on the other teaches more than something. It teaches some thing*s*. It does not discriminate by just teaching something to one or other of the groups. It teaches them both some things.

What it teaches the big guys is that more than brute strength is required in life. After all, what good is it to be able to throw a ball through a wall if you can't hit the little guy standing against it? Strength and size are wonderful, but only if harnessed with good eye-hand coordination. Big guys have to have good eye-hand coordination to hit a little guy. That's because little guys are good at avoiding being hit. For three reasons:

1. They are small targets. Remember, they are little guys.

2. They move around a lot at high speeds. This movement is a result of having lots of nervous energy. The nervous energy is a result of fear. This fear is a result of the big guys throwing the ball at them.

3. They don't like being blown through walls by balls and so use the other two to their maximum advantage.

If a big guy wants to really nail a little guy, he has to have a combination of strength and ability. He has to be able to make his hand throw the ball at the spot where his eyes see you. Then, and only then, will he be able to put you in the infirmary.

What it teaches the little guy is that size (the abundance of it that is) tends to make people arrogant. Size is tantamount to power. There is a saying about power tending to corrupt. Well, the little guy's motto is "Size *does* corrupt." Big guys know they are big and think that as a result of this glitch in genetic engineering they are somehow better than you. If they are better than you, that means they can do anything to you that they want to. So they do.

They pick you up and place you upside down in trash cans.

And laugh.

They get booster seats for you in McDonald's.

And laugh.

They smash you through a wall in gym.

And laugh.

Stuff Your Guidance Counselor

And it's all supposed to be okay. It is supposed to be their right just because they are big.

Whether it is right or not doesn't matter. It is just the way it is. You'd better learn that because it may have more meaning in your everyday life than does $E = mc^2$. It is a fact that will follow you all of your life.

Big people (or companies or cities or countries) think it's okay to take advantage of little people (or companies or cities or countries). So they will. And do. Unless, that is, you can show them why they shouldn't.

Which takes us back to my ancestor, Rabbi Leaking. You remember, when little David came to talk with him about the guys from Gath? There was an especially big one named Goliath.

David came to Rabbi Leaking and said, "Rabbi, Goliath is like a totally big dude and, while I'm really gnarly, I'm not so big. Like y'know, what should I do?"

Rabbi Leaking thought and thought and said, "David, my boy, you are little and Goliath is big, and since he's big he thinks he has the right to beat up on you, so . . . run for it."

Fortunately, David didn't listen to my ancestor. He listened to God.

On the surface, things didn't look good for little David. But David was small, so he was a little target and moved fast and didn't want to be annihilated. These things, and the fact that God was on his side, worked in his favor. While running around, he picked up some small stones and played some sort of ancient dodgeball of his own. As a result, not only was he not annihilated, he won the game.

This so upset Goliath that you could say he lost his head.

What made the difference for David was that God was on his side. David didn't minimize the size difference between him and Goliath. He couldn't. But God could. And since David trusted God, God did.

I know this is not quite the way the Bible reports the story, but it's the way it's always told at our family reunions.

The real point of this is that big guys and little guys can each learn something from gym class. They can learn that size, speed, and eye-hand coordination, while they may be nice, are not necessary. What is necessary is having God on your side.

The good news is that this is not all that hard to do. You see, He already is.

6

DEAR DR. LEAKING:

WHAT IS THE PURPOSE OF THE SCHOOL P.A. SYSTEM? NO ONE CAN EVER UNDERSTAND ANYTHING THAT IS BEING SAID ON IT.

MICHELE FROM MUNFORD, TENNESSEE

Dear Michele:

XABMFIMGMBIJFNBNBITHN, understand? You don't? Why not? It couldn't be that this answer sounds as if it were broadcast over a school sound system, could it? Of course it does. And the reason I made it sound that way is a very good one. I'm not going to tell you what it is, so you will just have to figure it out for yourself.

Okay, I'll tell you what it is. The very good reason that everything over the school P.A. sounds like it is being read by a gorilla with a mouthful of mashed bananas is

AXMNMDNAIENCNAKDJREM. Got it yet? You don't. I guess I'll have to get serious then.

Now pay attention. The reason school P.A.'s sound like that is so that you will be prepared for experiences you will encounter later in life. Like after school today, for instance. You know, when the last bell rings and you stroll calmly out of school, hop in the car (yours, your mom's, your friend's, or a complete stranger's), and head to Hardee's drive-thru.

What happens when you get there? First you pull up to the menu with the built-in microphone/speaker. Next the sign begins talking to you.

"Welcome to Hardee's, may I take your order?"

"We'll take two bacon cheeseburgers, three large fries, four Cokes, and a plain hamburger," you say slowly, clearly, and carefully.

Silence.

"Welcome to Hardee's, may I take your order?"

You try again. "Yeah, it's the same as before, two bacon cheeseburgers, three large fries, four Cokes, and a plain hamburger," you drawl out even more clearly and carefully.

"Okay," says the speaker. "That's two NMSUNNLA-ING, three MLJNNIUUHEKJNFLK, INJNGUBJIN Cokes, and a plain JYBGYOURHYREKP. The total for your order is NMOKHHNJHUBHL dollars and KJI-HJNE. Please drive to the front window. KNIHMBU-GENDV for MHUHBGGVD to Hardee's."

Of course you haven't understood a single word that the speaker spoke at you. Even some of the English ones. And if you weren't *really* hungry for a JYBGYOU-

Stuff Your Guidance Counselor

RHYREKP you'd just forget the whole thing and go home.

This is where the school, and its weird style of teaching you by using things that seem to make no sense, has come through for you again. The school P.A. has prepared you for this experience. All your many years of trying to make sense out of what was being said too loudly, too softly, too garbled, or with feedback screaming through it has paid off. You can now interpret P.A. Even though the sounds emitted at Hardee's were unintelligible to the human ear, your years of in-school training work to your advantage. Your ear may not understand or even recognize the sounds as patterns of human speech, but somehow you know that the girl at Hardee's really said,

"That's two bacon cheeseburgers, three large fries, four Cokes, and a plain hamburger. The total is $12.87. Please drive around to the front window. Thank you for coming to JOKSHDBNNMC."

So you missed the last part. You caught most of the rest of it, didn't you? That's what is important. You need to understand the essence of things. Hearing the meanings behind the words is often as important as hearing the words themselves correctly.

To make sense out of any announcement that comes over the school P.A. you have to learn to listen carefully and closely. Not just for the words but for the stuff behind the words. The meaningful pauses and the exclamation points. If you don't listen carefully and closely then you miss lots of things. Stuff that will really benefit you in your academic or social career. Like the announcement that the first five kids to get to English Lit class will get

Never Told You

A's for the year. Or lovely Laura LaPorte, the girl of your dreams, is still in need of a date for homecoming. Or that, on the one day your mom let you borrow her car to drive to school, they are about to tow away "a ZXYBCKLDmobile, license number NWDSYTP, which had its lights on and was parked in a handicapped zone" or something else equally exciting.

When you listen, really listen, you find there's a lot being said that's worth knowing. You find out things about clubs, special events, this weekend's game, and more.

Hearing what God has to say to you can be a lot like listening to the school P.A. Sometimes it seems to come across garbled. That's because you probably haven't practiced listening to Him like you have to the school P.A.

For one thing, you're probably not expecting God to talk with you. You say your prayers. And you think that's good. It is good. But there's more to talking with God than that. Somehow most of us have gotten the idea that praying is talking to God. It is—partly. More than talking to God, though, prayer is talking *with* God. There's a big difference between the two.

Think about all the times you have tried to have a conversation with someone who did all the talking. They went on and on and on, and you couldn't have squeezed a word in with a crowbar. You began to feel more like you were being talked *to* than talked *with*.

The same thing happens when we pray sometimes. We get so busy talking that we don't give God a chance to talk to us. You know what I mean. We tell God thank You for this and that, and ask for guidance to wisely choose which outfit to wear to school tomorrow and "bless

Stuff Your Guidance Counselor

Mom and Dad and baby brother and . . ." until "Amen." Then out go the lights, and God, who was just ready to say something to you, finds Himself cut off in the dark because you're already in dreamland.

It is true that God isn't always easy to hear. He's a lot like the school P.A. You have to listen carefully to hear Him. God often speaks in ways we don't understand unless we happen to be paying close attention.

God usually speaks very softly. That means we have to shut up to hear Him. We have to turn off our mouths, and TVs and stereos, and whatever else is blaring away.

So, Michele, the next time the school P.A. has you listening very carefully to what's being said, let it remind you to listen carefully to other things, too. Who knows. Maybe God will speak to you through the wind, a storm, some silence, or even the Hardee's menu sign.

"Let's see, you ordered a good life, peace of mind, and KJNIDJNNB."

I told you to listen *carefully*.

7

DEAR DR. LEAKING:

I HAVE A SCIENCE QUESTION FOR YOU. ARE THE ANIMALS IN BIOLOGY CLASS SUPPOSED TO BITE YOU WHILE YOU'RE DISSECTING THEM?

TIM IN TITONKA, IOWA

Dear Tim:
 No.
 You want more of an answer than that? Okay.
 No, they are not.
 How was that for more of an answer? Still not good enough, was it? Well, I'll give it one more try.
 No, Timothy, the animals you are dissecting in biology lab are not supposed to bite you. They are not supposed to be all pinkish gray and squishy on the inside either. But they are, aren't they?
 Let's look at the facts. When you get to the part of the semester where you are finally going to dissect some-

thing, Mr. Peterson, the biology teacher begins to prepare you. You learn all about formaldehyde, scalpels, and other necessary things. Then he pulls down a chart that contains an artist's rendering of the insides of the animal you are gong to dissect. Usually you get to work on a frog. The chart purports to show you what the inside of a frog is going to look like. It doesn't. It's not even close.

The chart you will see will be nice and neat, with all the organs in color and outlined and labeled. It looks a lot like the maps in the atlas Dad uses on trips. You know, the one with all the states in different colors and nice, neat borders. (My little sister Kathleen was so convinced that those maps were true representations of reality that when we went on our first trip out of Ohio she was disappointed when we crossed the state border and there wasn't a real —O—O—O— lying along the ground and Michigan wasn't blue.)

The diagrams they show in biology class have all the vital organs in nice pastels and all in a particular place. It's all very neat and clean and antiseptic.

If Mr. Peterson wanted to show you a chart resembling what you actually would see, you would be focusing on a picture of something that looks like your little brother's first experiment with the chemistry set, Mom's blender, and the late, lamented family cat. When you finally take scalpel in hand and cut into a frog, that is exactly what you'll find.

The diagrams that Mr. Peterson shows you are not reality. They are merely an opening to dissection. (Get it—"opening to dissection." Never mind.) Though not as graphic a depiction of a dead frog's gushy innards as Freddie Kruger would like, they are an attempt to prepare you for what lies ahead. The charts are kind of visual clues to what you are supposed to see. That they do not mirror reality exactly is beside the point. For one, they are only meant to be illustrative. To give you a basic guide. For another, if they were realistic you wouldn't slice into a frog. You'd be sick before the first slice.

Regardless of how little the charts resemble reality, as you make your first incision (if the frog doesn't bite back, that is) you will learn something. You will learn which one of those pinkish gray squishy things is the frog's stomach and which one is its liver and which one is your lab partner's index finger.

As for the critter biting you, who can blame it? Would you want someone (or, from the frog's perspective, some "thing") cutting *you* open—even if you were dead? No, you wouldn't. Even a poor formaldehyded frog deserves some dignity in death. So it bites you, even if it is just an unconscious, delayed nerve reaction.

Expect the unexpected. That's the lesson here, for nothing will ever be quite like you think it will be or were told it would be. This is an important lesson for you to learn.

Life will never be quite what you expect. Sometimes, when you think it shouldn't, it will jump up and bite you. And it will never look like you think it should, either.

That's where God can help. After all, He put it all together. The frog and life.

God has even given us a sort of chart to living. It's called the Bible. It is unlike the biology charts or Dad's road maps. I know that some Bibles come with charts and maps of Paul's trips, but God didn't write those parts, some other folks did. The main part of the Bible is not all those charts and maps—even if they do make interesting reading during a particularly dull sermon. The main part of the Bible is the story of how God interacts with His people. Who are His people, you ask? Well, in the Old Testament it is the Israelites and in the New Testament it's all of us.

The interesting thing about God's chart is that it shows life as it is. The people in there sometimes have fuzzy morals instead of doing everything right. The bad guys have some good in them and the good guys always seem to end up doing something bad.

That's what's nice about God's chart. It shows life as it is—real! And through the reality is a thread that is woven into it. That thread is that God, who made it all, is there when His people seek Him.

So take a look at God's chart. And don't be afraid to ask for a little guidance when you need it. This is one chart that will help.

8

DEAR DR. LEAKING:

WHY IS IT THE TEACHER ALWAYS CALLS ON ME WHEN I DON'T KNOW THE ANSWER AND NEVER CALLS ON ME WHEN I DO?

SCOTT IN SHALLOWATER, TEXAS

Dear Scott:
 The answer to this question is obvious. Let's take a few minutes and see if you can figure it out yourself. I'll bet you can. Just follow the steps below and see what happens.
 Relax and close your eyes. Now try to remember how many questions Mr. Thornhill has asked in Algebra I this past week. Have you done that? Good.
 Now, try to recall how many times you knew the answers to those questions. Finished?
 Now subtract answer B from answer A. Do you have

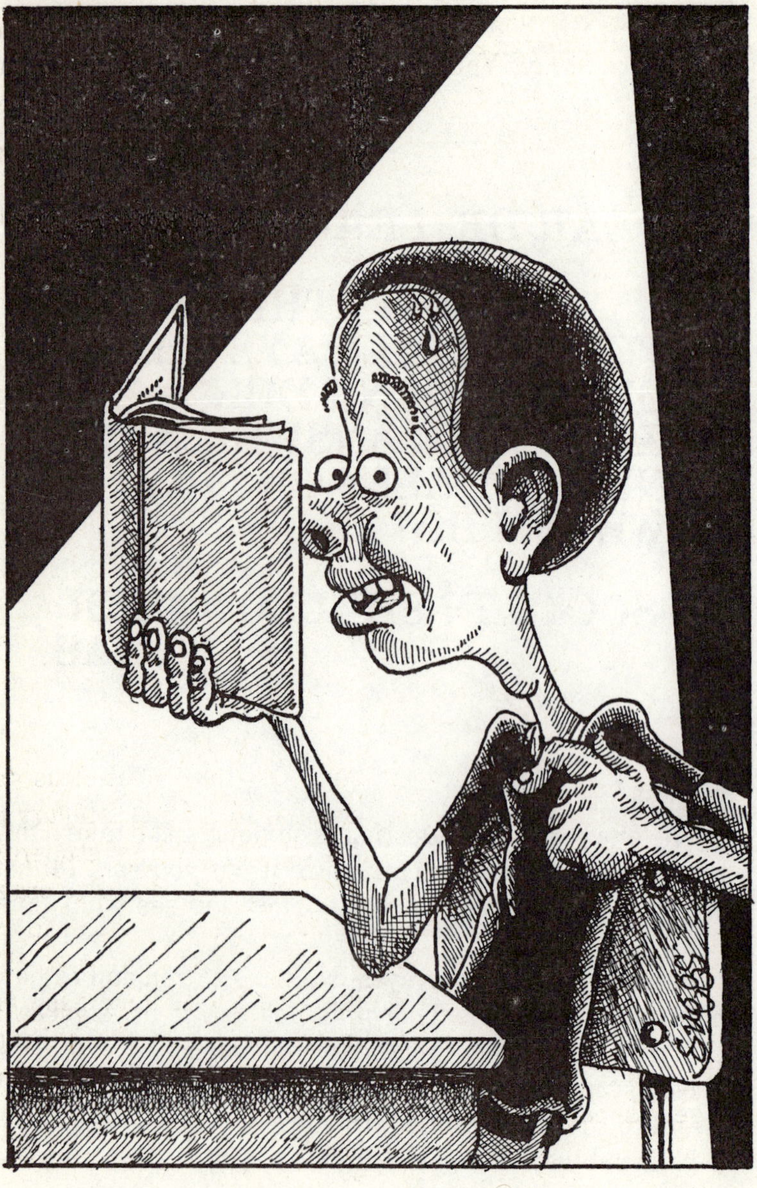

anything left over? I'll bet you do. Presto, chango, there's the answer to your question.

So you still don't understand? That's fine, we'll look at it another way. You see, chances are you did not know the answers a majority of the time Whether you were called on or not. That is why the teacher called on you when you didn't know the answer.

Teachers have an advantage. The numbers are working in their favor. Since you know the answers so infrequently, how can they do anything but call on you when you don't know the answer? They have almost insurmountable mathematical odds going for them. The law of averages is on their side. You do know what the law of averages is, don't you?

Well, just in case you don't (and about 75 percent of you don't, if you are really teenagers), here it is·

The Law of Averages

It is a law that the average teenager won't know answers when called on.

See, it's the law of averages—of which most of us are one. Average, that is. Most of us fall into that category in one or more areas of our life. We are average students, average looking, of average height, have the average amount of zits, and so on. So the above law applies to us. On an average day, that is.

So, with all this going their way, it is very easy for teachers to catch you when you don't know anything. And that's when you're paying attention. Which, averagely speaking, won't be very often. If they notice you

Stuff Your Guidance Counselor

staring out the window or contemplating Becky Brown's beauty, they've got you for sure. You can be sure you won't know the answer then, because you probably won't even know the question. Or that a question's been asked. Or what class you are in. Or ... well, you get the idea.

When that happens, prepare yourself for some major-league embarrassment. Teachers love to embarrass kids. It is even part of their contract, listed right after what subjects they are supposed to teach and what periods they don't have to deal with you. Some teachers only embarrass you because it is part of their contract. It's required of them, so they do it. They don't really want to, but they have to. Others, though, not only embarrass you because it is expected, they do it because they love to. They want to see you cringe and melt and squirm. They get great joy out of embarrassing you. In fact, there is only one thing that makes them happier.

That's when they can get you to embarrass yourself.

This usually is not hard to do. It is especially easy on those rare opportunities when the kid knows the answer.

How many times has this happened to you?

You are in class—in body, if not mind. It's a wonderful day and you've spent valuable time thinking about Jeff Ray's neat cherry red '56 Chevy coupe or Joan Stair's beautiful blue eyes. Mrs. Kirkpatrick's voice keeps dribbling down inside your ear, vaguely disturbing your musings when, suddenly ... hey, wait a minute! What was that she asked? It sounded familiar. Repeat it. Repeat it. *Please repeat it,* you wordlessly beg. I think I know this one.

"All right, class. We'll try this one more time. Now,

Never Told You

who can tell me what nation's capital city was named in honor of it's first president?"

Hey, I think I know that, you think, mentally running down all the national capitals you know. *Mexico City wasn't named after Señor City, and I'm pretty sure London wasn't named after Jack London. I know, Washington, D.C., after Thomas Jefferson Washington here in the U S of A.*

So you start waving your hands around. But so is everyone else in class. Why doesn't she seem to see you? Or everyone else who is having a fit? Why does she call on the one person in the room who is staring at his shoes, praying, *God, please don't let her call on me?* Why? Why? Why?

This is not all that hard to figure out. You should have a clue by now, at your age and after all your years of schooling. How many times has your waving your hands around caused a teacher to call on you? Sure they may have excused you to go to the boys' room because they thought you were about to flood the room. But they never asked you for the answer.

And the reason is—it's obvious you know the answer. You've given yourself away. Just as they can tell you don't know by the way you look at the floor when they're getting ready to call on you, so, too, can they tell when you do know by the way you're jumping around with your arm in the air. They might be old, but they are not dumb. And they know you know. By now you should know that they know you know. There's no way they are going to let you do something that would make you look smart.

Remember, they are adults and you are a kid. They are smart and you are dumb. They are the embarrassers and

51

you are the embarrassee. How can they embarrass you if they let you do something smart?

Sometimes they do it out of pity. After all, what would your friends think if you answer a question? They'd think you were pretty stupid acting so smart. "Who does he think he is," they'd ask, "Alfred Einstein?" Then they wouldn't talk to you for days for acting like you were better than them.

Life can be like teachers. It will rarely ask you a question you're prepared for. That's because you're rarely prepared. Lots of times you wander through life daydreaming. Just like at school. Occasionally you hear a question you think you know the answer to and so you answer it. But a good deal of time life just gets you as you are—ill-prepared. You haven't done your homework.

You need to take some time and think through the answers to the questions you know are going to come up. You already know most of the subjects. Drugs. Drinking. Sex. Cheating. Stealing. And so on. What are you going to do about all of these? Have you thought about it? Do you know where to go for help?

Let me suggest someplace. Actually it's Someone. Jesus.

You see, Jesus was a kid once. And the story of His life tells us He was tempted to do the same things you and I are. I know this sounds a little hard to believe. After all, this is Jesus we're talking about. He was the Son of God. It's hard for us to imagine Jesus and His buddies talking about whether or not to drink up their parents' wine and chase girls. It's hard for us to imagine Jesus had "buddies." The Bible does tell us, though, that He had to face the same desires we did. So, in many ways, Jesus was just like you and me.

In other ways He wasn't. For one, He studied up on life's questions. He was prepared when they got asked. He knew what His answers would be.

Jesus was the exception to the dumb kid rule. No teacher ever got the chance to embarrass Him with a question. As a matter of fact, you can even look up one time when He was caught teaching the teachers. As a kid! While that sort of stuff tends to give kids a bad name, I'm glad He did it. Because that means He can teach us, too.

So if you need help with life's questions and answers, ask Jesus. It's good to have Him on your side. He's already heard all the questions, knows you don't often have the answers, and is standing by ready to help. He remembers His student days and knows the answers you need now. So ask. He's one teacher who will notice all your squirming and turning and won't embarrass you.

Instead, He'll help you out.

9

DEAR DR. LEAKING:

I SIGNED UP FOR SPANISH AND FAILED THAT. THEN I FLUNKED FRENCH. AFTER THAT I GARBLED GERMAN. WHY IS IT THAT ALL FOREIGN LANGUAGES SEEM GREEK TO ME?

CHRIS IN CLAYHATCHEE, ALABAMA

Dear Chris:

¿No habla espanol? No sprechen sie Deutsch? No parlez-vous Français? Well, no problem. Hardly anybody else around here does either. To prove my point, take this little quiz.

1. What do you call someone who speaks three languages?

2. What do you call someone who speaks two languages?

3. What do you call someone who speaks one language?

Answers:

1. Trilingual
2. Bilingual
3. American

Since most of us fall into the category "American," question and answer 3 will apply to us. The fact of the matter is that to the majority of Americans, foreign languages are something that remain foreign. And a further fact is they couldn't care less. And an even sadder fact is that to many Americans our own language is a foreign language. Many people can't read it and millions can't seem to speak it. Especially sportscasters. People use double negatives or the wrong tense or verb conjugations. Maybe they don't like English because it was invented by the English who used to run the country a couple of hundred years ago and they haven't forgiven them yet.

We say that we want to learn to speak another language but that we can't. Maybe Americans do have some sort of genetic defect that prevents us from picking up foreign words and phrases. But I suspect that there's nothing wrong with our genes (after all, many of us have designer ones). I think that foreign languages are hard for us to learn because we don't want to learn them. The desire just isn't there. Why should we learn another language when most of the rest of the world is learning *our*

Stuff Your Guidance Counselor

language? Most everybody else in the world speaks English, don't they? Sure they do. Everywhere you go there's Pepsi, McDonald's, Cokes, and Kentucky Fried Chicken.

In spite of this there are still good reasons to learn a foreign tongue. There is a lot of joy in a foreign language if you take time to learn it. One reason you should learn another language is so you can be really funny. Even if you have not been successfully humorous in the past, if you can learn another language you can be a hit. You will be able to tell jokes that are understood only by the rest of the Spanish class. They will think it's really funny because it's in a language only they understand. Others will think you are funny, too. Mostly because of what they consider to be goofy sounds coming out of your mouth. Either way, people will laugh.

Learning a foreign language will come in handy when you go off to college, too. Greek could be especially helpful when you are wandering around an institution of higher learning. If you know Greek you will know whether you just joined a fraternity or a sorority. Of course, looking to see whether the membership is male or female should help here as well.

You will also appreciate being able to speak a foreign language as you get older and quit taking all your meals at Wendy's or Pizza Hut. When you are seated in a really fine restaurant, you can make quite an impression if you order *escargot* and don't start screaming "Waiter, waiter!! There are snails on my plate!" when your dinner arrives. If you can read a little bit of a foreign language, you won't ever end up eating raw ground beef by mistake. Like I did. Yum.

Of course, speaking a foreign language will be nice if

you ever visit the country whose language you speak. Thanks to your studies you will be a fountain of knowledge about the place. You'll know its culture. Its art. Its literature. And how to ask where the bathrooms are.

I've been to a foreign country. Trust me, that last one is the most important thing you can learn. You can forget how to say, "¿Como esta usted?" or "Parlez-vous Français?" Remember at all cost "¿Donde esta la cabana del baño?"

Learn a foreign language. While it may be a pain, and all look like Greek to you now, someday, with lots of practice and hard time in language lab, you'll be speaking Labrador like a native born Labradorian.

Some of us think talking to God is like learning a foreign language. We've heard people use all kinds of deep-sounding phrases and words we don't understand. They tend to do that in church quite a bit. Words like *sanctification, regeneration, catechism,* and more. And we've heard them often, so we think we know what they mean. But we would be hard pressed to use them correctly in a complete sentence.

So we don't talk about our faith very much. We think we don't know the language. We're not sure we can ever learn to speak it like our Sunday school teacher or the most Reverend J. Elton Bankerblood. We quit going to church or Sunday school because it's like going to a foreign country. We don't know what's going on, we don't speak their language and they don't seem to speak ours. It's just not much fun.

There's good news, Chris. You don't have to learn to speak "church-ese" or whatever it is many religious people speak. Jesus didn't. The Bible tells us that one reason the people of His day liked what He said was that they could understand it. He wasn't always trying to impress them with some highfalutin theological double-talk.

So if Jesus didn't bother to learn it, you don't have to either. Just get to the place where you let Him talk to you. Try it in church, even. Tell Him, "I don't understand what the Reverend Bankerblood's talking about." If it's important, Jesus will help you understand. If it's not, don't worry. Just listen to Jesus. He may have something more important to tell you Himself.

The moral of this story is—in life, learn another language. It will help you grow, and find the bathroom.

At church, use the language you already know. Jesus knows it, too.

10

DEAR DR. LEAKING:

WHY DO TEACHERS SAY THAT THE ONLY DUMB QUESTION IS THE ONE YOU DON'T ASK, AND THEN, WHEN YOU ASK A QUESTION, SAY THAT IT'S THE DUMBEST QUESTION THEY'VE EVER HEARD?

SHAUN IN SUGAR GROVE, VERMONT

Dear Shaun:
 Now that's a stupid question if I ever heard one!
 Is that the kind of response you get? Do your teachers actually say things like that? You didn't think I was saying that it was a stupid question, did you? Not a sensitive guy like me. No, I was just asking if that's the sort of answer you got when you asked,
 "Mr. Medley, is professional wrestling real?"
 Was good old Guido Medley understanding and help-

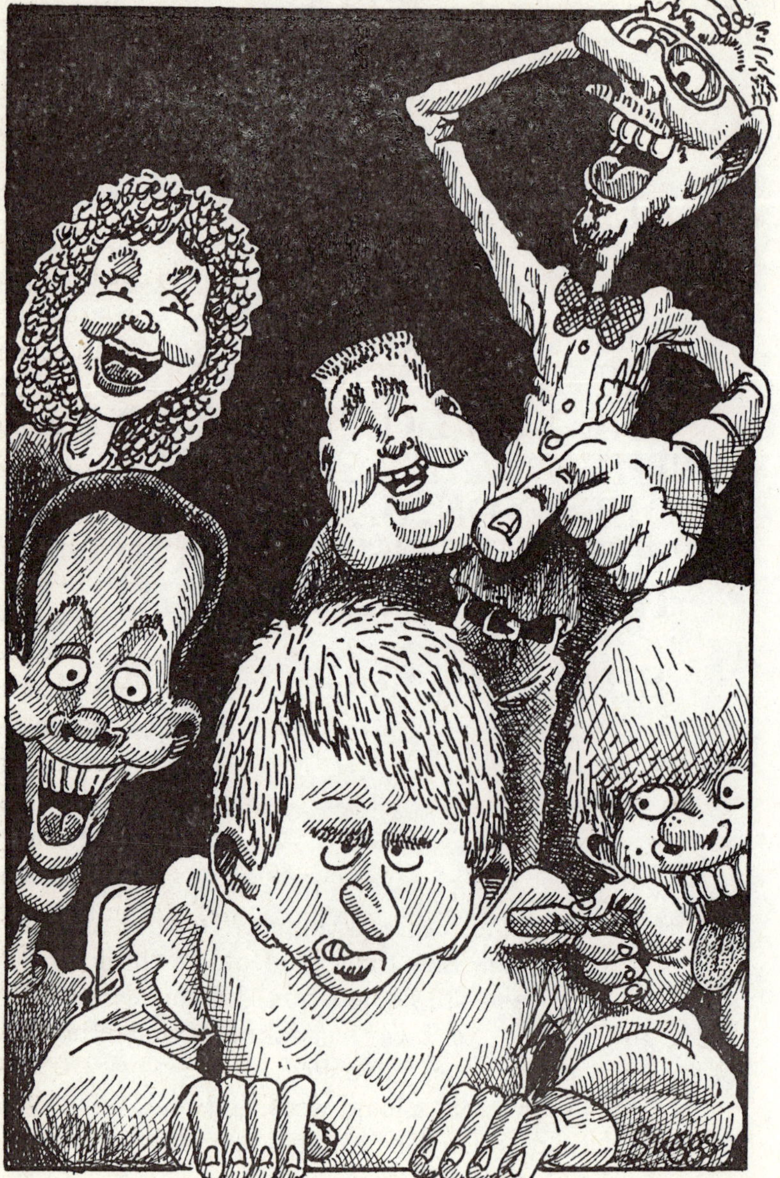

ful? Or did he say, "Now that's a stupid question if I ever heard one?"

If he's a real teacher, the chances are he chose the latter as a response. If he's a substitute, also known as an unreal teacher, he probably ignored you in an attempt to achieve his goal for that class period—to survive. And if he's a student teacher, also known as a practice teacher, laboratory teacher, or stupid teacher, he probably asked you what you meant by the question and then psychoanalyzed both you and your question, all the while trying to remember which teaching theory covered this situation. But we are talking about Mr. Medley, who began teaching there shortly after he graduated from college in 1787. He's a real teacher. So he replied, "Now that's a stupid question if I ever heard one?" And I'll tell you why he did. Later.

Before I do, however, let us examine the first part of your question. That is "WHY DO TEACHERS SAY THAT THE ONLY DUMB QUESTION IS THE ONE YOU DON'T ASK. . . ." They say that because they have to. It is mandatory. Most schools' boards of education require their teachers to say that at least four times a day. They have a very good reason for it. It's a legal reason. It's what's known as a disclaimer.

You know what a disclaimer is, don't you? It's when Frank Gifford says, "The pictures and events of 'Monday Night Football' are the exclusive property of the National Football League . . ." and so on. It's the statement that appears on the side of a pack of cigarettes reading "Warning, the surgeon general has determined. . . ." It's when your Mom yells, "You'd better quit making that face at your sister or someday it's going to freeze that way and then, boy, will you be sorry and don't come crying to me when it happens and your friends all laugh at you and...." Well, you get the idea.

A disclaimer is a neat little thing. Actually, it's two things in one, kind of like a Certs. ("It's a breath mint." "No, it's a candy mint.") At first glance it looks like some sort of warning. It appears that whoever is doing the disclaiming really cares about you and doesn't want you to get hurt or die or get in trouble. It is almost considerate. That seems nice. Your teachers don't want you to die ignorant, so they are encouraging you by saying that no question is too dumb. "Don't be afraid, ask away."

The second part of the disclaimer is the real reason for its existence in the first place. The first is a sort of camouflage. It's there to make you feel good and hide the real purpose. The second, and real reason for a disclaimer, is to protect themselves. ABC uses disclaimers because it wants a chance to sue your socks off if you use any of the witty repartee between Dan Dumbdorf, er Dierdorf, and Al Michaels and Frank Gifford. The cigarette makers use disclaimers because they don't want you to sue their socks off while you're dying of cancer, emphysema, or some other really bad thing. It protects them and makes it look like they care about you.

That's why the Honorable Association of Teachers and Educators Kvetching for Individualized, Demonstrable Schooling (HATE KIDS) came up with the disclaimer, "The only dumb question is the one you don't ask." It's not because they want you to ask a question. They pray you don't. It's just that they don't want to get sued by some parent whose kid never said a word in class because he was terrified that if he spoke up and said something stupid the teacher would make fun of him. By using the HATE KIDS disclaimer, they have an out.

"Hey, I told little Laura that it was okay to ask questions. Is it my fault she sat there like her jaws were wired shut?"

So that's the reason for the first part.

Now for the second part (WHY [do they] SAY THAT IT'S THE DUMBEST QUESTION THEY'VE EVER HEARD?). It's because they are smarter than you are. I don't mean they have more knowledge, in spite of their years of advanced education. What I mean is they have more street smarts. They are sharp, savvy, hip, and whatever else you can think of. And one thing that is imperative to being street smart is not to ever, *ever* look stupid.

What happens when a teacher asks you a question? The first thing is you realize you don't know the answer. The second thing is you get all clammy and cold and hot and sweaty. Then you mumble an attempt at an answer. Or pass out.

What do you think happens to a teacher when *you* ask a question? As hard to believe as it is, they are human. Most of them are, anyway. The first thing that happens is they realize, like you, they don't know the answer. And while *you* can get away with not knowing the answer—after all, you are the student and you are supposedly there to learn answers—they can't. They are the teachers. Not the teachees. They are the acclaimed fountains of knowledge. How can they say, "I don't know," or, "I'm sorry but the dog ate my lesson plans"? They can't. They won't buy excuses like that from you. How can they hope to get one like that past you? That's where the smarter than you comes in.

Stuff Your Guidance Counselor

They realize that they don't know and they don't want to look stupid. Being smarter than you are, they decide to make you look stupid. They say, "That's the dumbest question I've ever heard."

You immediately feel like a fool. You're sure that 95 percent of the rest of the class knows the answer and you—and only you—are lost upon the high seas of ignorance. All the while Mr. Medley is glaring at you as if you were an idiot. Which you are convinced you are.

That's smart. Mr. Medley has turned the attention from himself and his ignorance to you and your supposed stupidity. Now he doesn't have to answer the question he couldn't answer anyway. And he doesn't have to worry about your asking any more questions for a long time.

Asking questions is pretty scary. When you do it you run the risk of embarrassment. No one likes to be embarrassed. Especially by their own stupidity, whether it is real or imagined. In spite of that, asking questions is a good way to learn. And it is okay.

It's even okay to question things about religion. You are allowed to ask questions about why you've been taught the things you have about your faith. Why does your church believe __ about __ ? Asking questions may make your preacher, youth group leader, or parents uncomfortable. Some of them may even try to pull the teacher routine on you. People may question your faith if you have doubts or questions. Don't worry about it. That's their problem. You see, God doesn't mind if you ask questions. He even encourages it.

Jesus said He was the "Truth." If He was the "Truth," a little questioning is not going to make what He said any less true. So go ahead and ask. Investigate. Seek the answers to any questions you have about God, Jesus, the Bible, what you've been taught. It's okay. God can stand up to the scrutiny. God will never say, "That's the dumbest question I've ever heard."

God doesn't have to do that. He doesn't have any ignorance to hide. He knows the answers. He should. He wrote them.

11

DEAR DR. LEAKING:

WHY DO SOME KIDS GO TO CLASS EARLY?

RANDY IN ROMEO, MICHIGAN

Dear Randy:
That is something that has baffled me for years, too. I wish I could figure out a good reason for it. The only thing I can think of is that they missed about a two-week period in second grade. You know the section I mean, the one where they teach us to tell time. Maybe these people never learned to tell time. It could be that they don't realize they are early for class. If they have no concept of what time it is, then in their minds they aren't really early, are they? They're just there. And we're not. They probably can't figure out how come they are in their seats before anyone else is even coming down the hall. Perhaps this is all very disconcerting to them.

I hope it is. After all, people who show up early for things give the rest of us a bad name. They should feel bad about it, don't you think? For a number of reasons

One is it makes them look as if they are more inter

ested in the class than we are. This may be true. Okay, it not only may be true, it *is* true. Even though it's true, however, we don't want the teacher thinking they're more interested than we are. Even if she knows they are. It just makes us look bad, and we don't need any help doing that. We can make ourselves look bad all by ourselves. How can they live with themselves knowing they've made us appear as if we didn't care?

Another reason they should feel crummy is they take the front seats. This means, logically enough, that we have to take the back seats. This makes us look like we care even less than we previously appeared to care. Which was not much. Strike two. We don't get to class early and we sit in the back. How could we look any less interested than that? And where does Mrs. Cooney look when she wants to pick on someone? That's right, in the back. Where she assumes all the kids who don't care are sitting.

Teachers never look at anyone in the front rows. They are always gazing toward the rear where the supposed troublemakers and other disinterested parties are perched. They don't have to worry about the darlings in the first three rows. It's those buzzards in the back that they have to keep an eye on—and pick on by asking difficult questions like "What subject was I just addressing, Mark?" or "Let's see you spell *cat,* Penny."

Still another reason they should feel like bottom crude is that they have made themselves appear to be smarter than we are. Who would be fool enough to sit in the front row if they didn't know the answers? Not you or me. Or them. So they look smarter than we are because they are brave enough to be early and sit up front. Never mind

67

Stuff Your Guidance Counselor

that they probably are smarter than we are. That just annoys us more.

Finally they should feel terrible because what they are doing makes the teachers not like us. Teachers like people who get there early and sit in front and look like they know the answers. They're not nearly as fond of people who get there on time or late, sit in the back, and probably have the IQ of a newt. And we want—no, we *need*—Mrs. Cooney to like us. Her liking us may be the only thing we have going for us. It sure won't be our being on time. Or sitting up front. Or knowing the answers. Our only chance may be that she likes us and takes pity on us and passes us. After all, three years is too long to be in the tenth grade.

Those kids who arrive early do glean some real, and not just perceived, benefits by doing what they do. Those rotten kids get there in time to look over their notes before the quiz. Or get some clues on the lesson from what's written on the blackboard. Or even, hard to imagine as it is, talk to the teacher one on one, as one human being to another instead of the way teachers usually relate to you and me.

I suppose being early can have its advantages. Take the women who went to the tomb on that first Easter. They did not go because they expected anything good to happen, that's for sure. They thought Jesus was dead. They'd seen Him crucified. Instead of hiding out like the men, they went anyhow. And what a surprise they had. They got to be the first ones to find out about the miracle that had occurred. Not only was Jesus not dead, He was waiting there to talk to them. They were the first people to encounter Jesus after His resurrection. It never would have happened to them if they hadn't gotten there early.

So, while I don't really understand why some people always get there ahead of time, I guess it does have its benefits. By being early we may be able to witness things we never even imagined. We may be a part of something fantastically unbelievable. Who knows what surprises God has in store for us.

Come to think of it, I believe I'll leave now to grab a seat in the front row. Want me to save you one?

12

DEAR DR. LEAKING:

WHY, AFTER ALL MY YEARS IN SCHOOL, DON'T I EVER GET A LUNCH PERIOD WITH MY FRIENDS?

CARL IN CHOCOWINNITY, NORTH CAROLINA

Dear Carl:
Lunching with one's friends and companions can be one of life's most enjoyable experiences. To partake in a public, yet private, repast with one's comrades in education is truly exhilarating. There is lively conversation, exquisite edibles, and a special bonding that occurs while dining with friends. And Mr. Manners says that's precisely why the school never lets one have lunch with one's friends. Remember, you are not there to have fun, you are there to learn. So forget eating lunch with your friends, Carl.

Besides being unable to resist making you miserable, the school has deeper reasons for not letting you lunch with Alan, Terry, Teddy, and Bubba—though for most school administrators that would be reason enough. Those deeper reasons result from their knowing what would happen if you and your friends actually got together during lunch period. They are aware of the possible consequences of such an event and they're pretty sure they aren't ready for them

What usually happens whenever you, Alan, Terry, Teddy, and Bubba get together at any time? General mayhem (No, that's not the southern officer who lost to Grant at the Battle of Elkin and cost the Confederacy a victory in the War of Northern Aggression). The first thing that happens is you start dressing funny. You all put on loud Hawaiian shirts and stupid hats or some other nonsensical clothing. All of you that is except Neil, who doesn't want anything to detract from his designer jeans. Then you start acting weird. Ridiculous. Outlandish. You laugh a lot and giggle and do bizarre things.

The school principal knows all this. Do you think for one minute that Mrs. Hollingsworth is going to let you all get around food at one time? Think about it.

What happens when you get around food? Well, you start out eating it. So far so good. By the time you're finished eating it, though, someone ends up wearing it. That's because a lot of really strange things happen in the middle. You are silly in the best of times. Around food is not the best of times. When food is in the vicinity you get downright bizarre. Things you would never try at the dinner table at home (because Dad would kill you) seem worth doing. So you:

- Stick french fries up your nose and in your ears.

- Eat the french fries you stuck up your nose and in your ears.

- Unscrew all the tops on the salt and pepper shakers.

- See how many hot dogs you can stick in your mouth at one time

- Chew up your food, ask everyone who walks by "Do you like seafood?" and then open your mouth and display its contents while your buddies yell, *"SEE* food!"

- Try to make each other laugh while drinking so that you'll
    a. cough and choke
    b. drown
    c. or have milk come out your nose.

This last one is the most fun and is probably worth a week's detentions, as long as it's not your nose gushing milk.

Then there's the subject of food fights. You may not think teachers and cafeteria monitors are very bright, but they are smarter than you give them credit for. For example, they know that very few food fights are caused by warring factions like the Geeks versus the Greeks or the Band against the Boozers. School officials are very aware that most food fights begin among friends. They know that there is something about friends and food that makes french fries fly and sandwiches soar. So, in the interest of cleanliness and not wanting to scrape spaghetti off the ceiling again, they keep you apart.

Something special happens when friends eat together. The people at the school know that. It's not the kind of lunch special they like. Jesus knew it, too. In the Bible you can read about many times when Jesus and His friends got together over a meal. There was one time when He and 5,000 of His closest friends got together for some fish and bread. Some say what happened at that meal was miraculous. And He was always trotting off to someone's house to grab a bite. Like at Zacchaeus's place. There was another miracle there. Wherever Jesus and food got together it seems a miracle came along, too.

These miracles had a lot to do with people's lives being changed. Rich people gave to the poor. Thieves gave back what they had stolen—and more. Little people became bigger—at least inside. Other people heard God talking to them. Lots of things happened when Jesus and His friends ate together. Miracles seemed to be on the menu.

Miracles can still happen when Jesus comes to a meal. You can eat the bread and remember His body that was broken because of His love for you. Or you can take a drink and remember that He is the living water which quenches all your deepest thirsts. Jesus will be glad to dine with you at anytime. All you have to do is invite Him.

Jesus will even be glad to come eat with you, Alan, Terry, Teddy, and Bubba. You might even get through that meal without a food fight or nostrils dripping milk. Talk about a miracle.

13

DEAR DR. LEAKING:

WHY DO SCHOOLS HOLD TORNADO DRILLS? IF A TORNADO COMES OUR WAY, WILL I HAVE ANY CHANCE ANYWAY?

ROYCE IN RANSOM, KANSAS

Dear Dorothy, I mean, Royce:
No, you probably won't have a chance. Unless of course your little dog Toto is with you. The only chance you might have will come from reciting the following prayer:
"Auntie Em, Auntie Em, which art in Kansas, I want to go home. I want to go home."
Don't say this prayer very loudly in public, though, or your friends will wish you had a brain. Or courage. You better hope they have a heart.
So why do they hold tornado drills if you don't have a chance? For the same reason they held bombing-raid drills in the fifties. Back in the olden days, when nuclear bombs were still really scary, people used to practice

what they'd do when the crazy Commies sent their bombs raining down on the land of the free and the home of the soon to be crispy critters. They built little houses underground called bomb shelters. They stocked them with food and water and clothing and Ping-Pong tables. They figured that when the air raid sirens blew they would rush home to their little shelter, lock out all of the neighbors who hadn't had the foresight to plan for atomic holocaust and survive World War III. They'd simply let the bombs stop falling and then come out. Of course they'd have to wait a few months or decades, and there wouldn't be anything left to come out to. But they figured whichever side had the most people walk out of bomb shelters would be the winners of the war. What benefit there would be to winning such a war is hard to say, but nobody wants to be on the losing side.

So people built shelters in their backyards, stored food in the basements of high schools, and had the kids practice air raid drills. During these drills, the kids used to hide under desks or cover each other in the corridors (preferably away from glass windows), practicing for when the Russians would drop the big one. We all knew the Russians would drop it first. We wouldn't, because we were the good guys. Never mind the fact that we invented those terrible bombs first and were the only country to use one on another country. We would cower in furnace rooms or hide under desks, imagining endless fleets of Russian bombers overhead, piloted by atheistic maniacs preparing to unleash their burdens of billions of bombs, dropping doom on God's people. As if hiding under your desk or covering your "buddy" (who was usually some dumb girl you wouldn't want to protect in the first place) would save anybody from a direct hit by an H-bomb.

Then Intercontinental Ballistic Missiles (ICBM's) came along and made the whole exercise pointless. They were too fast to stop. The warning time vanished. Those babies would be in downtown Boise before you could make it under your desk, let alone down to the school basement or home to the bomb shelter.

Still we practiced and practiced. Until it became apparent that the Russians were probably just as afraid of us dropping ours on them as we were of them dropping theirs on us. Then we all quit. Maybe we got used to the bomb. We lived with it so long that it just wasn't as scary. Sort of like when you watch *Friday the 13th* over and over and over. Pretty soon it's not scary. It's just boring.

That's not to say nuclear bombs shouldn't be scary. They should. But they aren't. We have gotten used to them. So, even though we have enough of them to blow us all up five or six times each, we don't worry about them. No one has air raid drills anymore.

This is very disappointing to teachers. They enjoyed the drills. It's fun to watch kids diving for cover, trying to protect someone they have hated since kindergarten. Since it was fun, and you aren't very afraid of H-bombs going off at O. C. Moore Memorial High School (in fact you kinda wish one would) and can't be conned into being too scared about it, teachers had to come up with a new twist. Tornado drills was it. Tornados are almost as scary as H-bombs, kill you just as dead, are totally unpredictable, don't need to be set off by crazy Khomeinis or Commies, and have the added fear factor that every American kid who watches TV news has seen tornados tear up trailer courts a couple of times a year.

The neat thing for teachers is your hiding under the desk is no more going to protect you from a tornado than it would from a direct hit by an H-bomb. The sight of all your backsides as you huddle under desks, shielding some nerd from certain death, brings back fond memories of the Cuban missile crisis and other scary things from their past, however.

And what memories they are. The good old days. The days when it was better to die fried to a crisp in a nuclear holocaust than be a slave of the godless Russian or Chinese Communists.

See, there is safety in the good old days. You can't control the future, but you can control the past. It is easy to look back and imagine it was better than it was. You can convince yourself that life really was better back then. Especially when you are scared by the present and terrified of the future. Teachers and other adults love to look back. They have fond, if not accurate, memories of the past. The feeling is called *nostalgia*.

When you're a teenager you have reverse nostalgia. You don't look to the past for solace. There's not that much to look back on. Instead you look forward to the good old days of the future. The past is your parents and others telling you what to do, believe, think, and feel. In the future of your thoughts, you're in charge. Everything will be the way *you* want it. In your nostalgic future you have lots of money, a great car, a good-looking spouse, and a huge, beautiful house. You have a job you love, but don't need to go to since you are so rich. Everything is great. There are no problems in your future.

But just like your teachers' pasts are figments of their imaginations, so, too, is your future.

That's not to say it's not important to dream—or remember. It is. It is even more important to live in the here and now. The present is all you have. It is all God gives you. The past, even as short as yours is, is the past. It has faded away. The future is always the future. It never arrives. It never will.

You are always in *now*. You need to learn to live in it. That's what God intended. Jesus urged us not to worry about tomorrow. Tomorrow, He said, will take care of itself. And don't spend too much time looking backward. Remember what happened to Lot's wife when she decided to reminisce about life in the old hometown. She ended up a pillar in the community.

The next time it's tornado, fire, or any other drill time, remember why you're there. In case it's not a drill, the next few minutes may be all the future you have. And the past won't do you any good. Learn to live life in the *now* with the One for whom time is always *now*.

When you walk with God there is no time like the present. That's because for Him it always is the present.

14

DEAR DR. LEAKING:

DOES EVERYBODY'S LOCKER GET STUCK SO IT WON'T OPEN, OR IS MINE SOMETHING SPECIAL?

ISAAC IN INDIAHOMA, OKLAHOMA

Dear Isaac:

You will be glad to know that having a stuck locker is something that happens to everyone. I don't know why this answer will make you glad. But I figure it will since having a stuck locker seems to be of major importance in your life. Now you know you are not alone.

No one has ever gone through school without having their locker get stuck. At least once. Unless it is one of the really cool kids. Nothing bad *ever* happens to them, even something as minor as this. Since you are a normal type kid, you can be sure that your locker will stick on occasion. Well, actually it tends to stick to the frame, not on the occasion, which is not even part of a locker. What I meant to say was that you can count on your locker door becoming unopenable every now and then.

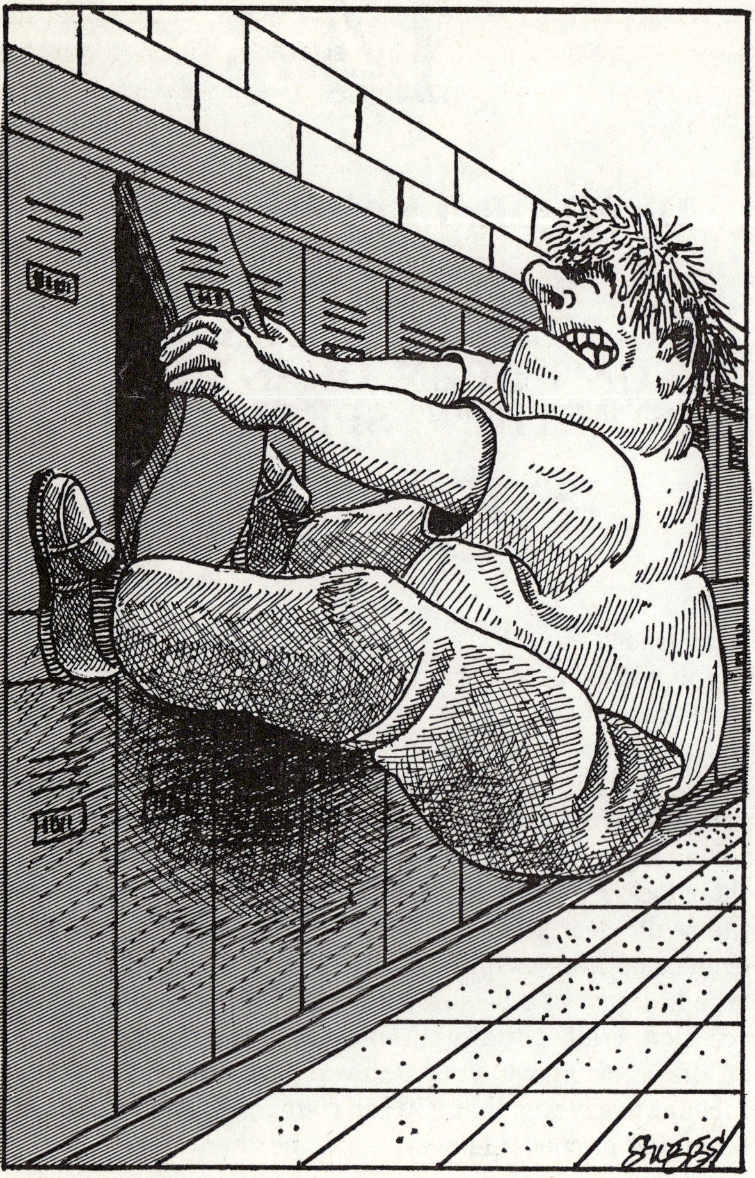

There is some good news. Though scientists have been unable to devise a way to predict earthquakes and tornados, they have come up with a set of criteria that allows them to predict locker sticking. Through careful analysis, numerous case studies, and minutes of research at the Leaking-Fawcett Institute for High School Studies and Plumbing, they have uncovered several commonalities of locker sticking. These studies have made it possible for modern scientists to construct models that allow them to predict locker sticking with a 99 percent degree of accuracy. Our hard-working men and women of science then rewrote their highly technical studies, putting them in your language so that you could make use of them yourself.

The Leaking Method of Predicting Imminent Locker Sticking

(These factors are reliable 99 percent of the time with an error factor of 95 percent either way.)

You may be reasonably sure your locker will stick if any one (1) of the following conditions exist. If two (2) or more of the following conditions exist your locker will definitely stick. If any three (1 + 2) of the following conditions exist, don't even bother to go to your locker.

Your locker will refuse to open if:

- You forgot the combination of the lock.
- You are late to class.

Stuff Your Guidance Counselor

- You are about to miss the bus.

- You get to school early, so that you will have plenty of time to get your locker open.

- You have a 12-minute lunch period and you carried your lunch that day and put it in your locker.

- The book you need for your next class is in your locker.

- There is anything at all you need inside your locker

There is another side to all this negativism. That is that your locker will always open easily when it is not necessary for it to do so. If it doesn't matter whether it will open or not, it will open. Easily. This is called the "It Just Doesn't Matter" corollary to **The Leaking Method of Predicting Imminent Locker Sticking.** Simply stated, the law is "If it has to, it won't, and if it doesn't have to, it will."

It will always open easily when it is stacked with stuff. Or when something like your jockstrap could fall out and really embarrass you. At times like that you don't even have to try to open it. All you have to do is walk by and it will open itself. In front of some nosy teacher. And all your friends. Of course, your friends will be very supportive and laugh at you all the way to the next class.

So what does **The Leaking Method of Predicting Imminent Locker Sticking** have to say about life and faith in God and other important stuff? It could be that when you're really depending on something or someone, you may be let down. People, like lockers, have a mind of their own. They also have something that lockers don't have—free will. So just when you count on people to stand up for you, and really need them to, it might turn out that they won't. The person you thought was your best friend might decide to act like a sticking locker and shut you out. You'll want to be inside, and even need to be inside, but he or she won't let you in.

There is only one Person you can go to that can always be counted on to be on your side. That's God. That doesn't mean He likes or approves of everything you do or say. He doesn't. Even during the times He hates what you do when you're screwing up, though, He still loves you. He will never turn His back on you. You will always have a place of safe haven with Him. In fancy church language that's called *grace*. Grace means that you can always count on God even when He couldn't count on you.

The next time your locker sticks or your best friend kicks you in your emotional teeth, remember—people and lockers will let you down. God never will.

15

DEAR DR. LEAKING:

WHAT IS THE NATIONAL HONOR SOCIETY AND WHY AIN'T I IN IT? I ARE A REEL GUDE STUDENT.

BEN FROM BOGALUSA, LOUISIANA

Dear Ben:

To answer your question, I'm going to start by asking you a question. I'll try to go slowly and make it simple. How do kids like yourself who want to play school sports know they are really good? Take a few minutes and think about it. Done? Okay, kids know they are good when they've made the varsity team. Not everyone gets to wear a varsity "M" from good old Mullenville. Only the best get to play varsity, right? The National Honor Society is a kind of varsity for those who are good at "mathletics" instead of athletics. These kids are mathletes instead of athletes. They would rather do layouts than lay-ups. If they are going for the long bomb, they're building one—not throwing it.

I know it is hard for you to believe, but there are some kids who do not excel in athletics. They will never be good enough to make the reserves, let alone the varsity. Some can't even play intramurals. There are some kids who can't dribble a basketball, throw a football, lob a tennis ball, or dodge a dodgeball. It's sad, I know. How are they supposed to lead a normal life? You feel really sorry for them.

In spite of this grave lack of athletic ability, these children are worth something all the same. They do have something that they can contribute to society, even if it won't be the perfect spiral or a new high-jump record.

Many of these kids are really smart. Instead of practicing headers they've been using theirs. You shouldn't hold this against them. In most cases, they can't help it. It's not something they did. Or even want. It's genetic. They were born with the potential for real intelligence. And at the stage of life when the hormone was triggered that turned you into a combination Bo Jackson and Reggie Jackson, they had a hormone spurt that made them a young Mr. Wizard. Their brain swelled up like your biceps. They absorbed information like you did Absorbine, Jr. They limbered up their minds while you limbered your muscles. They got all *A*'s while you got . . . well, you get the idea. It was something that happened to them like your being born with great musculature happened to you.

Sure some of them are smart, you say. But they study. That's why they are smart. That's partly true. Some of them do study. However, studying for them is not the same as studying for you.

For one thing you hate it. Your parents have to make

Stuff Your Guidance Counselor

you do it. Your folks have to lock you in your room with your books and not let you out until you have your homework done. They, on the other hand, like it. I know that's hard to believe, but they do. They go straight to their rooms when they get home and do all their homework right away. And then they do more reading so they can get extra credit.

Studying for them is what practicing is for you. You may have natural ability, but you still need to develop it. So you practice and practice and practice. You stretch your body to its limit so that you can get the maximum performance from it when you call on it. All your practice gets you to places you never could have reached otherwise. When you have finally developed that perfect throw that only comes from endless practicing, you feel really good. Great even.

They get the same from studying. The same thrill you get when you've reached the limits of your athletic ability and succeeded, they get when they finally grasp the illusive concepts behind advanced trigonometry. Studying is their practice. Tests are their games. An *A* is their varsity letter.

See, to them, it's what they do best. We do some things better than other things. Everyone does not excel at everything. We all tend to specialize. We work at what we are naturally good at because we realize we have the most potential for success there, not somewhere else. That's okay.

God made us each one different. Some of us are smart. Some of us are athletic. Some of us are both. They aren't mutually exclusive. But we are all different. In spite of that difference we can all be in the Olympics—be they special, regular, or academic. That's what's nice about being different. Being different doesn't determine worth. The athlete is not any better a person for being an athlete than a scientist is because he's a scientist. What we do doesn't determine what we are worth.

What does determine our worth then? Our unique human-ness. We are all unique and all have great potential for good. God gave us that potential. What we do with the talents we have is what makes us worthy individuals. God wants us to be the best we can be. With practice—be it mathletic or athletic—we will be.

So even though you ain't goin' ta git in Honor Soceity, Socitea, ah heck ... Club, don't worry about it. You are who you are. That's honor enough. Just be glad you are Ben. I am.

16

DEAR DR. LEAKING:

IS THERE ANY WAY I CAN BREATHE IN THE REST ROOM?

BERT IN BEECH BOTTOM, WEST VIRGINIA

Dear Bert:

I assume by your question that you are referring to the noxious odors, mostly human in origin, in the bathroom and have not in fact forgotten what your nose and lungs are for. If you are one of those rare humans who, some time since your first human encounter of being hung upside down and smacked soundly on your little bare bottom caused you to suck huge quantities of air into your lungs, has forgotten how to breathe, I'm not sure I can help. For one very good reason. You are dead.

On the other hand, if you are alive, and I assume you are since your letter was not postmarked *Cemetery,* your question is probably dealing with the aforementioned (and smelt) odors. This can be answered. To do so, however, we need to lay some very basic foundations of knowledge. We need to set the stage for the play of life.

We must plow the fields to grow crops from our seeds of education. We gotta start at the beginning.

By now you have probably noticed that the bathrooms at school are nothing like the ones at home. For starters, there isn't anyplace to take a bath. That's why schools don't really have *bath*rooms. At school, bathrooms are known as rest rooms. Though this would seem to be a mere exercise in semantics, with the nomenclature interchangeable, it is not. Just why it is not is illustrated below.

Let's say you're at school.

"You're at school."

No, no. I didn't mean for you to say "You're at school." I was speaking figuratively. What I meant was, imagine that you are at school. While sitting in biology class you feel a need to perform a certain biological function. The teacher catches the frantic look on your face and inquires as to the difficulty. You say you need to go to the bathroom.

Mr. "No Such Thing as a Stupid Question" Peterson (remember him?) asks, "Why? Do you need to take a bath?"

If he misses this golden opportunity, don't worry. Your friends won't. When you get back they'll ask you, "How was the *bath* water? Did you wash behind your ears?" We all appreciate such loyalty in our friends.

Likewise, if the call of nature strikes at home and your reply to "Where are you going?" is "To the rest room," your siblings and parents will taunt you with such witty sayings as "Why? Are you tired?" or "Do you need a rest?"

There is no real good comeback to either of these fas-

Stuff Your Guidance Counselor

cinating statements other than to graphically describe what biological function you intend to perform upon your arrival at (a) the bathroom or (b) the rest room. And you shouldn't do that because if you give in to this temptation you will not find yourself going to (a) the bathroom or (b) the rest room. Instead you will be going to (c) the principal's office or (d) your room. Both of which only serve to enhance your need to go to (e) the bathroom or (f) the rest room.

Besides the names, there are other differences. The most noticeable difference is that at home, the place where the aforementioned unmentionable biological functions take place does not have a noxious haze hanging in its atmosphere. Unless, of course, your father just left there. In that case, turn on the exhaust fan and call the EPA. After two or three days the pollution levels should be low enough to permit your return.

As bad as the smog at home is, school is worse. At school, you can hardly see through the haze that your kindly fellow students have hung there for you. This is both a blessing and a curse. You don't really want to see through the stuff because most school bathrooms are really disgusting. The usual regard for hygiene that is inbred in most teens is flushed down the toilet at school. The place is a mess. Disgusting. So the haze hides that. That's not all bad.

But it's not all good either. Since the rest room is so disgusting, you want to do what you came there to do and leave as quickly as possible. It's hard to find the necessary hardware in a "pee" soup fog. Thanks to that haze it's difficult to find your way around in there. It's even harder to find your way out. When you look at it objectively, the haze is more curse than anything.

You can't see and you are afraid to breathe. All because of that stuff hanging in the air Thank your fellow members of the esteemed student body of Mullenville High. Do they care? No. This haze is a direct result of their violation of the no smoking rule. It doesn't matter to them. Why? Because they have a better chance of not being caught smoking in the bathroom than they do in Mrs. Gallien's accounting class. The only one who smokes in there is Mrs. Gallien. And that's only when someone forgets to make a proper journal entry. Then it comes out her ears. So the kids smoke in the bathroom.

This is not something new.

Smoking in the bathroom has been a problem ever since the Indians showed "thee" Pilgrim kids what to do with rolled-up dry leaves and some matches from the *Mayflower*'s kitchen. They did this mostly to aggravate our forefathers and foremothers, who invited them to Thanksgiving dinner in gratitude for their help in getting through those first nasty winters, and then stole their land when they fell asleep watching the Lions-Cowboys game on TV after the dessert course. The Pilgrim's rooting for the Cowboys didn't help the relationship, either.

So what's a person to do? Both the past and the present are against you. That's the bad news. The good news is that there are a number of alternatives. One is to practice holding your breath. Check out a book on deep-sea sponge diving. Read it carefully and thoughtfully, paying close attention to the detailed instructions concerning the practices of the breathing (or is that not-breathing?)

techniques contained therein. Or bop down to Mr. Video and check out *The Big Blue* It's a good flick about sponge diving and has a couple of neat cars and lots of guys and girls in bathing suits. Just do what the divers do—except for the one who dies. Pretty soon you'll be able to hold your breath for 37 minutes or seconds, depending on how much of the video you watched.

A second alternative is to rent a Self-Contained Underwater Breathing Apparatus for the duration of the school year. This is also known as SCUBA gear. Not "Scooby-Doo," SCUBA gear. Though they sound alike, there is a difference. "Scooby-Doo" is a cartoon show that steals all the oxygen from your brain while SCUBA gear gets it *to* your brain. Since the oxygen you breathe while using SCUBA gear comes from a sealed tank and not from the outside atmosphere, it can also come in handy when you're going through the cafeteria line.

Finally, there is prevention. No, there is no way to prevent the haze in the bathroom. Prevention here means preventing the reason for going in there in the first place. This consists of following some fairly simple guidelines. In fact, there's only one: "Do not consume anything from midnight to 4:00 P.M. Sunday through Friday." Follow this rule and you'll never have to go to the school rest room. You could say it eliminates elimination.

Life is sometimes like the school rest room. It can be full of things that stink. And it's often hazy, too.

When it gets that way you need to ask God for some help breathing. He's had a lot of experience helping people keep their head above water. Just look at Jonah or Paul.

Peter got a helping hand from Jesus when he started

going under. And not just out on the Sea of Galilee, either. Sometimes we need help clearing the air. We need someone to help us get past the smoke and ash of life and breathe cleanly. Confusion is a part of life. But we don't need to stay lost in life's fog. We need to look up to where God is, above the mess we've often made for ourselves.

So the next time you're lost in the men's room, Bert, look up above the haze. Maybe you'll find an answer God has for you. It may look just like the top of the exit door. Thank God you can breathe again.

17

DEAR DR. LEAKING:

NOW THAT I AM IN HIGH SCHOOL, THERE SEEM TO BE SO MANY CLASS CHOICES. HOW DO I KNOW WHICH ONES TO TAKE?

EVAN IN EAGLE BUTTE, SOUTH DAKOTA

Dear Evan:
There are a lot of class choices today, aren't there? Back in the old days, students didn't have the difficulty you have. There weren't that many classes. The reason is that there wasn't much to study. Let's look at some examples from the past.

1 million B.C. Trog starts school at 8:00 A.M. He can't study Language Arts—there is no language or art. He can't take history either because there isn't any. Trog is home by 8:01 A.M.

Third Century B.C. Euclid goes to school in Greece to

study math. He can't take geometry because he hasn't invented it yet.

A.D. **1863** Ebenezer Sitler, student at the Spiceland, Indiana, Academy, hears the words *Gettysburg Address* and thinks of a street number in Pennsylvania.

You get the point. Time marches on. New subjects for study are born at an alarming rate—at least for the poor students who have to study them all. It used to be simpler. There wasn't as much to learn, so there weren't that many classes. People learned the Three *R*'s, no not rock 'n' roll and root beer. Readin', 'Ritin', and 'Rithmetic. Never mind that the last two don't start with *R*. Spelling was not one of the Three *R*'s.

Today there is a plethora of pedantic possibilities confronting you. There are subjects you need to learn that weren't even thought of 30 years ago—like "America and the Post–Vietnam War Syndrome" or "Programming the IBM Model 30." Back then Vietnam was some little country in the Far East that no one cared about and IBM just made business machines.

When you get to high school you find yourself in a situation where confusion reigns—and rains. In fact it pours. You are caught in a storm of studies. Unlike grade school where your teachers decided which subjects you would study, you are now thrust into situations where you have to make choices concerning what classes you are going to take. You have an important resource—your guidance counselor. Just how he or she can help you will be discussed in the next chapter.

For now, though, you find yourself alone, adrift upon a sea of indecision, surrounded by hostile class descriptions with nowhere to turn. What's a person to do?

There are several ways you can find your way back to shore safe and sound. I wish I knew some of them so I could share them with you. I don't. The only thing I can do is let you in on some of the more popular methods of filling out a schedule. It's sort of a guide to the common ways of choosing classes. Included in each description are some of the pros and cons of that particular method.

Period Method

This method consists of determining how many periods of class time you have to fill. You then pick the courses alphabetically and by times offered until your schedule is filled in.

Example: You have nine periods in a day. You need to find six academic classes. You only need six because you have one lunch period and two study hall periods. The only hard part of this method is deciding where to put the lunch and study hall periods. These need to be strategically placed as it is in them that you will accomplish many of your major high school tasks—visiting with friends, getting nourishment, reading *Sports Illustrated* or *Seventeen,* and writing notes to your friends. Put your lunch period in fifth period, one study hall in third and the other in ninth. This gives you an early break, a midday luncheon, and a rest at the end of the day. This last one is especially important because it's where you will dream up the reasons you tell your folks you had such a rough day. You then have to find classes for periods 1, 2, 4, 6, 7, and 8. Begin with period 1 and the letter *A*. Find a class that begins with *A* that meets during period 1.

Then move on to *B* and period 2. Then 4 and letter *C*. And so on.

This is an easy and practical method. It does have one drawback. If you do not skip around in your handbook of course offerings, you may end up taking a semester's worth of classes from one department. Your schedule might end up looking like this:

Thomas, John Alan   Home Room 103

Class:
1. Art: An Introduction
2. Basic Painting: Watercolors
3. Study Hall
4. Color: The Friend of the Artist
5. Lunch
6. Drawing: Exploring Pen and Ink
7. Exercises in Silk Screen
8. Study Hall
9. From Fabriano to Fromentin: Famous Artists Whose Last Names Began with *F*

This is probably okay if you are planning on majoring in art, but it's bad news if you want more of an education.

Easiest Course Method

This is similar to the Period Method except you are free to roam around the alphabet. You cast off the restrictions of order for the freedom of locating the easiest courses. You still begin by looking at the number of periods you have to fill and then computing the lowest number of courses you can possibly get by with to fill those slots. This method of course selection is a little more creative than the previous one. You can be bold and daring. You can take courses you never dreamed of, as long as you remember the object. That object is to not sign up for anything very difficult. Look for the easy classes. You will always choose "Addition: How to Do It" over "Trigonometry."

The main disadvantage to this method is that you generally need some upper level courses to graduate; so if you use this way exclusively throughout your high school career, you may find yourself hanging around for a year or three after the rest of your class graduates. It can be a little embarrassing to watch your friends graduate while you complete your fifth year as a junior. But hey, by the time they make you graduate or put you on staff, you will really know addition.

What You Like Method

If you use this method you will choose only those classes that interest you. This is an easy method to use if you like lots of things. It is difficult only if you are a real boring person who doesn't like anything. What makes it hard is that you do have to choose something. If you don't, the school administrators will choose for you. And you probably won't like what they choose. That's the drawback to this method. That and the fact that there aren't too many schools offering classes in "Tanning" or "Hangin' Out and Lookin' Good."

The Best Method

The best method is simply taking a variety of classes from each of the main subject groups—mathematics, English, science, social studies. This way you will gain knowledge in a lot of areas. It could help you discover which area excites you the most so that you can choose a career path you will enjoy. Plus you will learn a lot of things about a lot of different subjects. This will help you win big at Trivial Pursuit tournaments.

Then choose some fun electives as sort of dessert for your day. These can be things you really think might be fun, but don't want to major in. Things like art or music. Who knows, after taking them you may decide you want to be an artist or musician. If you do, you'll have a basis for talking to people about your music or calculating how much to charge for your latest sculpture in the light of recent economic trends as you interpret them from historical sequences similar in nature. Or whatever.

God used the Best Method when He created us. He made a wide mix of people. He made tall ones, short ones, fat ones, skinny ones, and more, all coming in a wide range of colors and with varying skills and degrees of interest. He used a common theme of love of family and friends. He provided us with basics in appreciation for the arts—be they music, paintings, or the colors of trees in the fall. But in spite of the core commonalities, He allowed for some variation. There is a theme around which we are built, but look at all the differences there are. I guess that shows us that God thinks variety is good stuff.

So stretch yourself while choosing classes—and life's experiences. Don't always take the easiest, or what you like, or alphabetical life. Learn to appreciate variety just as God does. Branch out and grow. You'll be glad you did. So will God.

18

DEAR DR. LEAKING:

WHAT CAN I EXPECT FROM MY GUIDANCE COUNSELOR?

ASHLEY FROM ASSINIPPI, MASSACHUSETTS

Dear Ashley:

You can expect a lot of things from your guidance counselor. Unfortunately, help won't be one of them.

While that would seem to make "guidance counselor" a misnomer, it doesn't. You have made two critical errors in logic when thinking about guidance counselors. The first is in the type of guidance you think you will get. You have assumed that when you visit your guidance counselor you will come away from the meeting with sound advice concerning classes, colleges, or life in general. Your definition of guidance is too narrow. Guidance does not have to consist of meaningful dialogue with a well-informed teacher-type to be guidance. An armful of college catalogs and a heartfelt "Ask your parents" is also guidance. It's guiding you away from blind reliance on the word of an adult and into the world of independent

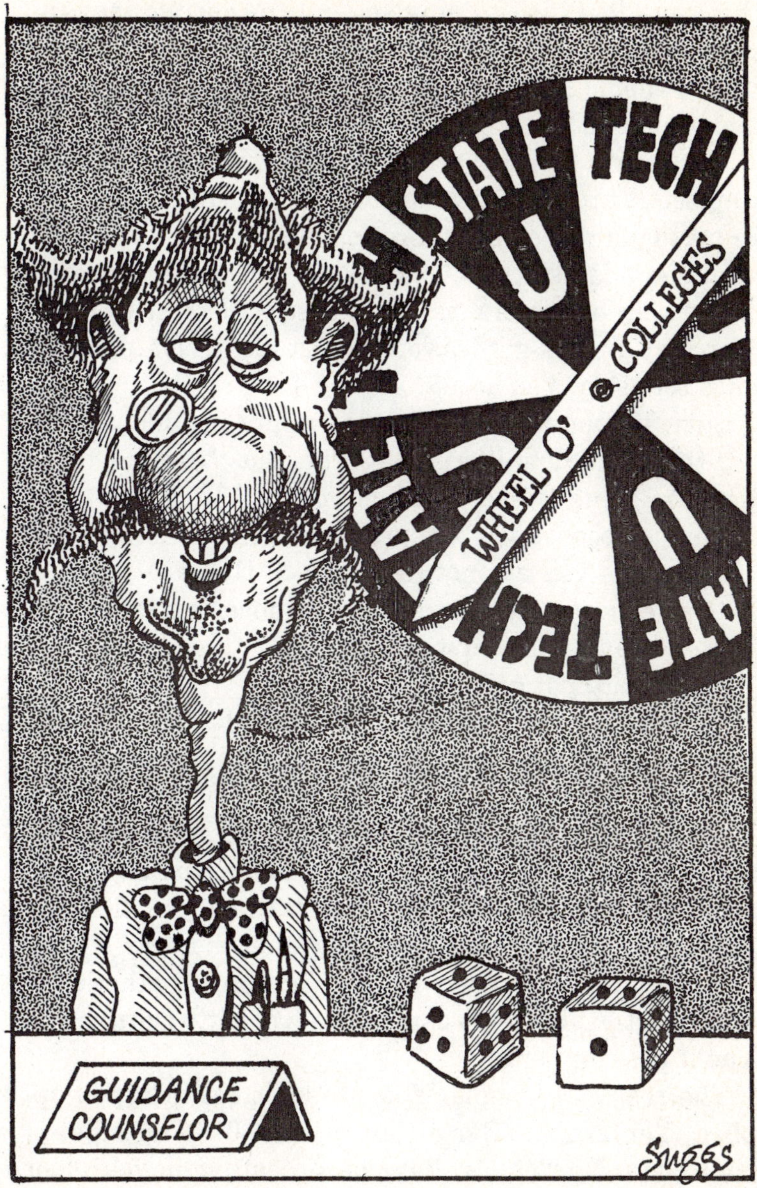
STATE
TECH
U
WHEEL O' COLLEGES
GUIDANCE COUNSELOR
SUGGS

thinking. It is also guiding you out the door so they can get back to reading *Guidance Counselors Quarterly* (this issue's theme is "How to be an effective counselor while avoiding kids").

Your second critical error is in thinking that guidance counselors are there to help you. Not kids in general; you in particular. They are there to help students. You have assumed that since you go to the school, sit through classes, do homework assignments (well most of them, anyway), and get grades you are a student. Not to a guidance counselor you aren't.

Sure, if you pressed them they might include you under the broad definition of *student*. But there is no way they are going to ever think of you as a student.

This is because you are probably a fairly normal kid. That means you are not (a) going to Harvard or (b) in special education classes. Just for novelty's sake, let's look at the first one first.

A. You are not going to Harvard.

You, Ashley, are a normal (whatever that is) teenager. You are smart, but not a genius. You are dumb, but not retarded. You study sometimes and goof off other times. Your grades are good, but not great. You get a lot of *A*'s and *B*'s, but the occasional *C* slips in now and then. You are planning to go to college, but when you think of *league* you think of Big or Pac 10 rather than Ivy. Perusing potential profferings from Princeton is pathetically unproductive. Better beg off on Brown. Ditto Dartmouth. You'll pass on Penn.

The reason is simple. You wouldn't get in if you applied. You aren't, after all, in the top .00005 percent of your class. No "Yalies" have been beating on your door begging you to come east and make their *alma mater* matter. Moonies maybe, but not Yalies.

If you were one of those few kids who had the potential to get into Harvard, you would find guidance counselors giving you all the help you want. And more. For one reason and one reason only. That reason is not because it helps you. It's because it helps them.

Think about it. Which of the following reports would warm a guidance counselor's heart (if he had one) and would make him look good?

"For the school year ending 199X I helped 27 kids get accepted into Jenny's School of Beauty, 42 into Bob's College of Diesel Mechanics and Truck Driving, 137 into New Castle State, and 16 into the armed forces."

or

"For the school year ending 199X I helped 4 of our finest young people gain admission to Princeton, 3 to Harvard, 2 to Yale, and 1.5 were accepted by M.I.T."

Is there any question?

It's not that there's anything wrong with the first one. It's just that everyone expects that 27 will go to Jenny's, 42 to Bob's, 137 to New Castle State, and 16 into the army, air force, navy, or marines. They'll do that without any help from Mr. Guidance. So, to make it look like he's doing a superior job, he has to spend most of his time with those brainy types who will go to Yale and get all *A*'s, win Rhodes scholarships and study at Oxford, and then decide it was all a waste and withdraw from society to wander around Europe and live in youth hostels for the next ten years.

His only chance to look good while sending someone to New Castle State is if the someone he sends ends up

Stuff Your Guidance Counselor

playing starting linebacker for Coach Woody Schembeckler. That's okay, too

Since you're going to go to State on something other than an athletic scholarship, and the only chance you have of seeing Harvard is when it plays Yale on TV, you are just not smart enough to get much help.

On the other hand, you are also too smart to get much help.

There are some kids in school who make you look like Einstein. Those are the kids who are in "special classes" or whatever it is that your school calls them. I am sure you know which kids I am talking about. They are the kids everyone calls names and makes fun of and pulls mean tricks on all the time These kids don't have to worry about going to Harvard, they just want to be able to get a job someday They want to do something constructive with their lives. They want help.

They need help because they cannot figure things out I don't mean the same way you can't figure things out. These kids really can't figure things out. Letters all run together when they try to read. Numbers are a foreign language they'll never comprehend. Not much seems to make sense. Their lives can be a hell that you should be thankful you don't have to endure. And it's not their fault. They just ended up that way.

These kids need assistance just getting through life. You may think you need help, but these kids show you how little help you need. They'll get help from the guidance counselor because it's the only chance they have to make anything out of their lives. Someone has to take time to help them put together a plan that will work for them. Sure it may be just to get a job at a sheltered workshop after high school. For them that would be as great an achievement as graduating first in your class would be for you

You are too smart and not smart enough, all at the same time. You're probably not going to get too much help from your guidance counselor. At least the one at school. There is another One you may have forgotten about. God.

The Bible tells us that we can get a lot of guidance from God. Acknowledge and call on Him and He will direct your paths, it says. That sounds like a guidance counselor to me. God wants the best for you. And He knows that no one needs Him more than you do. Since He made time, He can make time for you

When you're looking for guidance, call on the great Counselor. Appointments are available at all hours. For everybody. Especially you

19

DEAR DR. LEAKING:

WHAT STUDY AIDS SHOULD I HAVE?

KEN IN KNOCKEMSTIFF, OHIO

Dear Ken:
I'm glad you asked that question. Having the proper study aids on hand is very important for a student. The hard thing, as you've discovered, is knowing which ones are essential. Personally, I always thought the most important study aid I could have would be a genius for a classmate, a seat next to him or her, and 20/20 vision at test time. Just kidding. Cheating is not a good study aid.

So what are some good study aids? Below you will find a short list.

Essential Study Aids

1. *A compass.* Everyone needs a compass. It will help you draw perfect circles in your notebook or on the back of the person in front of you. It can also come in handy in geometry class.

2. *A dictionary.* You do know what a dictionary is, don't you? If not, look it up. Okay, so it's a thick book that lists lots of words and their origins and meanings. This can be interesting reading during a really boring class or when you just have time to kill. You can have all kinds of fun with a dictionary. And amaze your friends at the same time. For example, did you know that *phlogiston* is a word? It is. Look it up. See what it means. Have fun discovering the bizarre.

3. *A thesaurus.* This is a book that is kind of like, similar to, resembles a dictionary, but isn't. It is a book, volume, tome, dissertation of other words for the word you are using when you want to use another word. Confused? Unsure? Lost? I hope, wish, pray, you are getting the idea, concept, thought by now, presently, currently. A thesaurus is really handy for lots of things. It is especially helpful when someone calls you a name and you want to call him a name, but he is bigger than you and will kill you if you put it into language he can understand. Wise use of a thesaurus can transform "You big ape" into "Thou gigantesque, colossal creature of the species orangutan." Then he'll have to get a dictionary to find out what you called him. You'll be long gone by the time he looks it up.

I realize the above list is brief, but it contains only the essentials. These are the aids that everyone needs. You may take some classes that have special requirements. Art class usually requires things like paint, pens, ink, paintbrushes, and other arty stuff. These are definitely study aids you should acquire. Likewise, if you are in band, it might be handy to gain access to the instrument

Stuff Your Guidance Counselor

you are supposed to be playing. A trombone can be an essential study aid.

Accounting students should probably purchase some ledger sheets, lots of pencils, and even more erasers. Those who are taking French may want to buy a French-English dictionary (unless of course you are French and then you would want to buy an English-French dictionary). If you are signed up for golf you might want to buy some clubs. I've always been partial to Pebble Beach and Augusta, myself.

Study aids can be of great help or they can be a distraction. You can get so busy using your protractor to figure the exact angle you need in order to place a spitball between Mrs. Sexton's eyes, that you forget to use it for the problem on the board. Or you are so engrossed looking up *interesting* (that's one of the synonyms for *dirty* in the Teenage Thesaurus) words in the Spanish-English dictionary, that you forget you were supposed to find the Spanish word for *house*. Which is *hacienda*. ¿Donde esta su cabeza?

We can get so wrapped up in the fun of the things that we forget why we have them in the first place. An aid is just that—an aid. A help. Not the end all and be all. It's there to help make learning a little bit easier. Used properly it can make learning more enjoyable.

There are a lot of study aids for school. There aren't so many for life. There are a few, though. Two of them you won't want to use. I'm not saying you shouldn't use them, you won't want to.

Even though you won't want to use them, they are two of the most valuable study aids available. And they are not hard to find. They're your parents. Believe it or not, parents do have a good bit of value as a study aid for life. Some of that value comes as a result of the fact that they've lived it for so long. They've had the class before. They can give you a lot of information on making choices and avoiding the mistakes they have made. Talking with them about life is a lot like reading your older sister's notes from her English class two years ago, now that you are taking the same class. They can give you an edge.

Your parents can help a lot if you will let them. I know that is not a very popular thought, but it is true. In most cases they want to help. And in most cases you do have two parents. Even if they are separated or divorced. Your parents still love you and want to help, even if they don't live with you. It may be killing them inside that they aren't always at home with you when you need them.

Sometimes, if you have stepparents, you have even more study aids available to you. There are that many more places to go for help.

The final study aid for life is God. Your parents are good. God is great. The One who put it all together is there to help you make sense of it. What better way to study can there be than to talk with the One who wrote the book?

20

DEAR DR. LEAKING:

WHAT QUESTIONS SHOULD I ASK IN CLASS?

AMANDA IN ATHENS, GEORGIA

Dear Amanda:

I'm surprised you want to ask any questions after reading the answer to Shaun's question. We all know how stupid you can be made to feel for asking a question. But you are obviously of hardy stock and willing to endure much in your quest for knowledge. While I can't help you with specific questions, I can impart to you one good rule of thumb: Ask only questions that pertain to the class you are in at the time.

Let's look at this further. Many questions run through your mind while you are sitting in class. Questions like "How come Mr. Tridle has all that hair growing out of his nose and ears but doesn't have any on top of his head?" or "Why do they call the color blue *blue?*" or "If the light fixtures suddenly broke loose from the ceiling, just who in the class would be killed and become instant heroes on the six o'clock news?" or "Is Dave going to ask me to the dance or not?" and on and on and on.

Yes, you often have a lot of questions during class. It is just that most of them have nothing to do with academics. Teachers like to think you are there to learn what they are trying to teach you. Since the chance of any of the above questions having anything to do with the class you are in is remote at best, avoid asking them. You don't have to stop thinking them up. Just don't ask them out loud.

Occasionally, though, you will actually have an academic question pop into your mind. I know this is a rare thing. But sometimes, while you are sitting there thinking about Dave and the dance, something else will force its way into your brain. You may actually come up with a question like "How do I figure the square root of 25,473.23?"

"This," you say to yourself, "is an academic question. I am in an academic environment. I am a budding academician. Therefore, the question meets the criteria. I can ask it."

So far, so good, Amanda. You've mapped it out fairly well. But there is still one more test. Are you in a class that happens to be studying the subject about which you have the question? Or did you come up with a math question in German class?

You see, it is generally regarded to be bad form to ask your German teacher how to figure the square root of 25,473.23. There are two reasons for this.

The first is that you are in German class to learn German. You are not there to learn how to find the square root of 25,473.23. That's for math class. I realize that this

Stuff Your Guidance Counselor

may be a difficult concept to grasp, but it is true nonetheless. If you want to learn to scream "Attention!" the teacher will tell you to holler *"Achtung!"* If you need to know how to say "faster, faster" you will be instructed to say *"schnell, schnell."* Of course, you can also learn these simple phrases by watching TBS's "World War II Night" because these are about the only things the Germans say in war movies.

You can learn how to say other useful and exciting things in German class. Things like "There is snow in the street" (*Die est snie ein die strasse*), which can be particularly helpful if you are caught in a blizzard in Bonn. You will not, however, learn the square root of 25,473.23 in German class. Unless of course you phrase your question something like *"Was ist die rooten squaren ein 25,473.23?"* That's a long shot, though.

The second reason it is bad form to ask that question in German class is that Mrs. Schmeiser doesn't know the answer. After all, she took that math class when she was your age, some 50 or so years ago. Like you, she forgot how to do it as soon as the test was over. How in the world can you expect her to know the answer now?

Not knowing the answer makes her look stupid. Like a *dummkopf*. Whatever you do, you don't want to make a teacher look stupid. So, before you ask any question in any class, ask yourself, "Does this question have anything, however remote, to do with the subject the teacher's rambling on about?" If it does, ask away. If not, ask not.

There is a place you can ask any question at any time. That's where God is. Since you are with God all the time, even if you aren't always aware of it, that means you are

Never Told You

always in a place where you can ask questions. And further, since God is certified to teach in all subject areas, there is no question you can't ask.

Yes, any question is fair. How come really good people get cancer and die and bad people make lots of money and live it up? Why are little children starving? Where is heaven and what's it like? How come Mr. Tridle has all that hair growing out his nose and ears and none on his head?

You can even ask how to figure the square root of 25,473.23.

God will be glad you asked. He's always happy for a chance to share with you. And He has lots of answers. The square root of 25,473.23 won't be hard for Him. After all, He invented it.

21

DEAR DR. LEAKING:

WHAT DO I DO IF I DON'T LIKE A TEACHER OR CLASS?

ROBIN IN RIO ARRIBA, NEW MEXICO

Dear Robin:
This is a hard question. What makes it hard is that there are so many answers to it. And, as you will see, even though there are many answers, there aren't many good ones. This is sad. What is even sadder is that there will come a time when you get a teacher or class you don't like.

Having a teacher or class you don't like is one of the very few sure things in life. There's not much you can count on in life, except that you'll die and that you'll have a teacher or class you hate. Probably not in that order, though it may feel like it.

The object then is to keep this experience to a minimum. Think how bad it would be to have lots of teachers and classes you didn't like. Your life would be a lot like the plot of the movie *The School Year From Hell*. It's bad

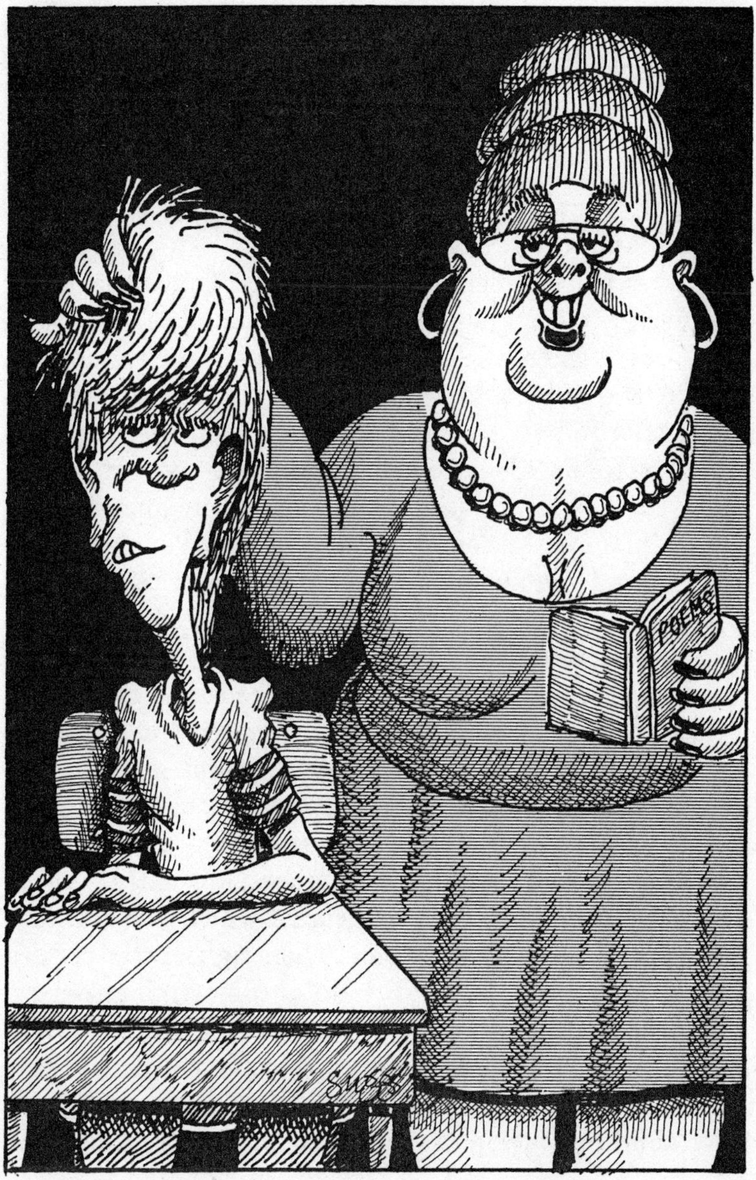
POEMS

Stuff Your Guidance Counselor

enough getting up each morning to go to school when you have classes you have some interest in and teachers who aren't terrible. Your mom may have to pry you out of bed with a crowbar now. What would it be like if you hated every class and teacher? Dynamite wouldn't get you out from under the blankets. Therefore, the recommended thing is to try to prevent having teachers or classes you don't like in the first place.

This is more difficult than it sounds. That's because it involves work. I know, I know. I shouldn't say *work* in front of a teenager. It's kind of like swearing in front of a priest. The sad fact is that it is going to take some work, some effort on your part, if you want to avoid the pitfall of our problem. Begin by spending minutes in research. Poll your friends, relatives, siblings, and anyone else you can think of. Ask them which teachers and subjects they recommend you avoid. Keep records and formulate a detailed list of their comments.

You will need this detailed list because you'll find that there isn't a teacher or subject that someone doesn't despise. When you've finished your research you are going to have to go back through your list and see who and what is least hated and who and what is most hated. This is not as much a matter of choosing from a plethora of positives as it is avoiding the numerous negatives. Having this chart helps you determine which subjects and teachers you stay away from. Then sign up for classes and teachers with the least hateful comments as recommended to you by people you trust.

Avoid guidance counselors at this point. Their priorities and focus are completely different from yours. You'll find that they have you signing up for classes and people who will actually be challenging to you. The ones they choose would help you grow intellectually. They'll stretch your horizons. You could even wind up doing lots of homework and reading and writing reports. If you don't watch out, you could actually come home from school at the end of the day having learned something. I can't emphasize this enough. Stay away from guidance counselors.

If, after all your careful study and planning (and avoiding guidance counselors), you still end up with a teacher or class you don't like, then you have a problem. That's the bad news. Now you have to figure out what you are going to do about it. You have several options. They are listed below.

Option 1. Quit school. While drastic, this is effective. If you quit school you do not have to deal with this dreaded teacher or subject again. Of course, you won't have to deal with a lot of other things either, like a job, a paycheck, going out on dates, or anything else that requires money. Very few employers are looking for high school dropouts for important positions. And the chances of $10 million coming your way are very slim, no matter what Ed McMahon says.

Option 2. Cut class. The big question here is whether or not you can hold your breath in the bathroom for an entire period. (See Bert's earlier question.) Forget about the *F* you'll get. Your grade point average never mattered before. Besides, lots of kids with GPAs of .49 graduate, don't they?

Option 3. Tough it out. This last one, while not the most attractive, is the best. It has a lot of advantages. The first is that you will get credit for attending class if you get a passing grade. And, as you know, I lied when I said lots of kids with GPAs of .49 graduate. They don't. And you want to. Graduate, that is. Regardless of how much you like the inside of your favorite classroom, you don't want to be sitting there long after your friends have gone off to college or jobs.

The second advantage is that you might even learn you like something you first thought you hated. An example. My wife, Nancy, has been trying for years to get me to eat mushrooms. Mushrooms! My opinion is that anything that can grow in your lawn should either be sprayed or mowed. But, being the nice husband I am, I tried them. To make her happy. Okay, to get her off my back. Then something awful happened. I liked them. All those years of hating them came back to haunt me. Mostly because Nancy kept saying, "I told you you'd like them. Didn't I? I told you."

Mushrooms are not as bad as I once feared. I use them a lot when I cook. Trying something I hated taught me a lesson: You can learn something from an unpleasant situation, too. The teacher you started out hating (or fearing or whatever) may turn out to be the best teacher you ever had. This happens lots of times.

My high school art teacher scared me to death on the first day. He was mean and surly-looking. And his attitude matched. But he knew art. And he really liked kids—he just hid it real well. Mr. McLinn became one of my favorite teachers (though I never told him that). I ended up taking every art class I could get. I even decided to major in art in college. And graduated with high honors in it. All because of a teacher I didn't like when I first met him.

You may learn that you are really interested in a subject you once avoided. Chemistry may be intimidating at first. Until you find that you have a special aptitude for it and go on to excel in it.

There are lots of times when we'd like to quit school or cut class. That's true in life, too. Sometimes life is rough, with lots of people or subjects we don't like. Just like hanging in there in school sometimes pays big benefits, so can hanging in there in life. How many times have you ended up as friends with someone you couldn't stand when you first met him or her? It's happened to me lots of times. And there are also things you are called to do in life that at first seem to be something to be avoided. Like washing windows or raking leaves at an elderly person's house. *It would be a lot more fun to watch Saturday morning cartoons,* you think to yourself. But watching cartoons doesn't make you feel as good about yourself as helping someone and ending up with a friend. Besides, some old folks are really cool.

So the next time you are facing something that you just want to avoid, don't drop out. Ask God for strength to give it a try. You might like it.

22

DEAR DR. LEAKING:

WHAT IF I'M LATE FOR CLASS?

MEGAN IN MANZANOLA, COLORADO

Dear Megan:
This all depends on how strict your school is. In some school districts, tardiness is punishable by death. I know that sounds horrible, but it's true. If you are tardy you will be assigned to a chair in the cafeteria and served a tray full of food from the menu. It is meant to be a slow and agonizing death. That's to teach you a lesson. You can bet after punishment like that you'll never be late again.

The good news is that those states also have an automatic appeals process. If you can get a good lawyer the appeals may take two or three years to go through the courts. During which time you will have your freedom and can continue to stay in school. Which means you will probably still graduate with your class. Of course, there's always the possibility your appeal will be turned down and you'd be executed the day after graduation. That's the chance you take by being late to class.

The idea of the death penalty for tardiness has generally been dismissed by most schools in this enlightened age. Sure, they may feel like killing you, but putting someone to death sort of defeats the whole purpose of their being in school. It's hard to learn when you're dead. You should know. Just look at some of your classmates. They've been dead in their seats for years. So, for the most part, unless you live within the confines of the Oskaloosa, Iowa, School Corporation, you will live to be late another day.

There are still lots of things that will happen to you if you are late. Though they won't mean that life as you know it will end, there may be times when you wish it would. Let's look at a few of them.

Generally the least that will happen is that everyone will stare at you and make you feel like an idiot when you walk into class. For some of us this is not all that painful—or unusual. There are lots of times when we walk into class and feel like idiots. We're sure everyone there is smarter than us and staring at us. The smarter than us is easier to take. That's because they probably are. There's a good chance that they know who Jean Baptiste Massillon was and why he's important. For some reason—probably because we haven't done our reading or homework—we don't.

It's the staring part that is difficult. We wonder what's wrong. Is our shirt buttoned up wrong? Don't our shoes match? Oh, no, our fly's unzipped! Nope, it's in the up-and-locked position. Maybe they aren't staring at us after all. Then why does it feel like they are?

The only time the other kids are staring at us is when we are late. They aren't staring because they think we are awful for being late. Most of them would like to be late, too. It's just that they are in the presence of an adult. And not just any adult, but the adult who controls their grades. And their grades control whether or not they get the car this weekend or have money to go to the movies or countless other things. So while they want to be you, they have to look like *they* want to be there and are anxious to get on with today's lesson and *you* are depriving them of valuable class time. You know how it is because you do it, too. Anything to win points with the teacher.

If you are lucky, the teacher will feel that being stared at by your classmates is agony enough. He or she won't say anything, knowing the punishment of your peers has caused you severe mental and emotional anguish. That's if you are lucky. Chances are you won't be.

That's because Miss Conn, the teacher, will really be upset at you. Angry. Mad. Ticked off. She has spent days and months and years preparing the lesson plan for this particular class period. This is the best one she has ever written. She's sure that when this period ends, the entire class will spontaneously leap to their feet, give her a standing ovation, and carry her triumphantly down the hallway amid shouts touting her academic prowess and teaching ability. Miss Conn has just begun her glorious introductory remarks. The class is enthralled—she can tell by the way they are staring at her all glassy eyed. Some are so taken in by her oratory that their mouths are dropped open in mystification. Of course, anyone else would notice that they are all dazed from boredom or asleep. They are semicomatose. But Miss Conn sees a class spellbound by her teaching. Then you wreck it by walking in late.

The class turns to stare at you. Even the sleeping have awakened. To Miss Conn the mood has been broken. It will never be recaptured. It is gone. And it is your fault.

This is one of the times when school prayer is acceptable. Even the Supreme Court agrees on that. You better be praying that your school system doesn't practice capital punishment for tardiness. If it does, Miss Conn is going to do everything in her power to make sure you get the cafeteria.

If you know something like this might happen, you may even consider cutting class. You think that it would be more helpful to the possibility of your continued existence to hide out for an hour. You think it might be wiser to do that than face the wrath of Conn.

Nothing could be more wrong.

The only thing worse than ruining a great teaching plan is missing it entirely. Here are the questions Miss Conn will ask as soon as she sees you next:

"Who do you think you are?" (If she doesn't know, don't tell her. It may be your only chance.)

"Do you think you don't need to learn this material?" (Of course, you think that, but take my word for it, it wouldn't be wise to mention that to her.)

"What makes you someone special?" (It could be your bright baby blue eyes, but I wouldn't mention that to her either.)

Skipping class will not help. You have to go. Even if you are going to be late. If you think you may be going to be late, keep in mind this simple rule: **Don't be.**

Stuff Your Guidance Counselor

Sometimes you just can't help it, though. The way schedules are, unless you are traveling by Concorde, you just won't make it in time. So let me give you some guidance on how to enter with the minimal amount of damage possible. First we'll look at the wrong way. See if you can determine why this is not the best possible approach.

"Yeah, I'm late, so what? Who cares about this crummy class anyhow?"

Figured it out yet?

There is another way that may get you into class without being glared to death and even win you some esteem in the eyes of the teacher. Try this method the next time you are late:

> "I'm sorry I'm late, Miss Conn. I was just so impressed by _____'s [last period's teacher] discourse on _____ [last period's subject] that I lost track of time and so am late to your class. I am sorry. So sorry. And he [or she] is not half the teacher you are. You are so much more interesting than she [or he] is. I hope I don't get so engrossed in your presentation that I'm late to my next class also."

This can work for a number of reasons. First, it makes you look as if you thirst for knowledge. It makes you appear as if you just couldn't tear yourself away from the drinking fountain of education. "Aha," Miss Conn says, "here at last is a serious student."

Also you made Miss Conn sound like a better teacher than last period's teacher. This ensures that your fabrication of the truth (also known as a *lie*) won't be discovered. That's because teachers very rarely get together and say things like, "Megan says I'm a better teacher than you are, Sinex. Nyahh! Nyahh! Nyahh!" Even if they want to.

If you practice this technique until you sound sincere, you'll have it made.

The only real drawback to being late is that you might miss something important. Like the answers to the questions on the upcoming midterm or something that could be exciting to know. Lots of things go on in class that could make a difference in your life, if you're there to hear them. So be on time. Get all out of class that you can.

There are times when we are late for life, too. We sleep away hours of Saturday morning. Or we lie around the house doing nothing because we're "bored." Meanwhile, there's plenty going on in the world. God has given us a life where there's lots to do if we want to. Every day there's a ton of things that need to get done—and someone to do them. Poor students need tutors, hungry people need food baskets prepared, homebound elderly people need visitors.

There are basketball games that need to be played and malls that need to be shopped at. There's plenty to do in God's world. From the really important to the really trivial. But regardless of which it is, it is there for us to get out and enjoy.

Don't be late—for school or life. God wants you to get as much out of life as you can. Besides, if you are late you'll never know what you missed.

23

DEAR DR. LEAKING:

WHAT IF I MISS A CLASS?

DAN IN DELIGHT, ARKANSAS

Dear Dan:

I hope you are not planning on having a career that requires thought, like being a doctor or anything. Did you miss the whole previous question? Do you remember one of the main points—do not skip class? Being late is bad enough. And here you are asking what to do if you miss a class.

If there's a possibility of the death sentence for being late, what do you think is going to happen if you miss completely? Do you think they are going to sentence you to two meals in the cafeteria? If they can execute you with one, they are not going to feed you two. That would be overkill.

You don't even want to know what will happen to you if you are unlucky enough to miss a class. It's too horrible to describe in a book like this. Let's just say that Freddie

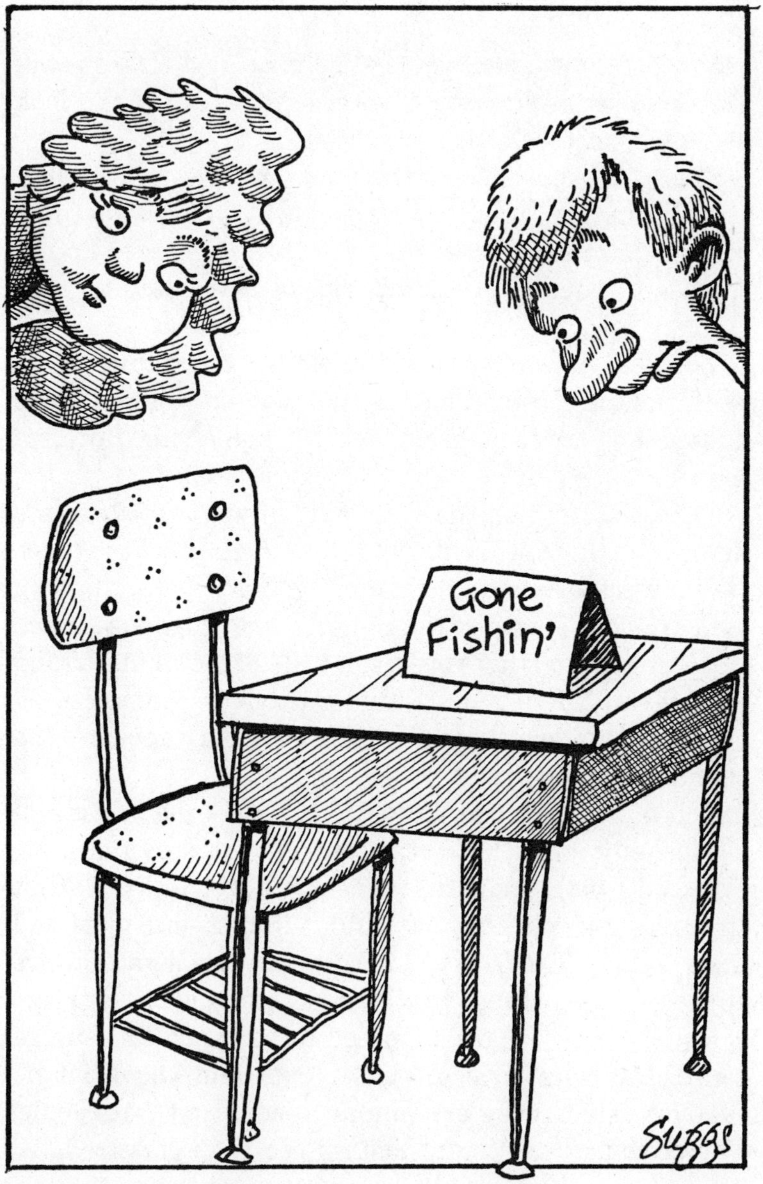
Gone Fishin'

Stuff Your Guidance Counselor

Kruger, Jason, and Leatherface would all like to be a part of it.

So what do you do if you end up missing a class? There are a number of things that *seem* logical. Let's take a look at them, shall we?

Thing 1. Apologize to the teacher. Give an explanation, no matter how lame, about why you were stupid enough to miss class. Make sure that it is true. Do not compound your original mistake of being late by also being a liar.

Thing 2. Inquire as to the possibility of making up the work. Ask if you may have any handouts you may have missed. Be sure to mention your willingness to stay after school.

Thing 3. Mention that you will be sure to secure class notes from those students who sit at the front of the class. Be sure to state that you are not going to bother asking your friends. They don't take notes; they just pass them.

Having looked these over, can you tell me what's wrong with them? There is one fatal flaw that is common to all of them. They may seem logical. They may appear to be sound. But they aren't.

The major flaw (no, he didn't fight at the "Battle of Elkin," either) is that these were invented by teachers. You and I both know that teachers never tell you what they really want. They say things that seem logical and make sense. That's because they are teachers and are supposed to say things that seem logical and make sense. They, themselves, are supposed to be logical and make sense. But when has a teacher ever told you what he really wanted. They are human. They don't want logic. They want *blood*. Yours. You missed their class.

Never Told You

If you really want to be forgiven, make up the work, and keep on living, you need to do the following:

Step 1. Walk up and down the hallway in front of the classroom you should have gone to, wailing, "Unclean! Unclean! Woe is me! Woe is me! Unclean! Unclean!" This first step is important because, as far as the teacher is concerned, you are unclean. You are scum. You are bottom crude. You missed their class. By acknowledging that you know what they know and agree with it, you may have a chance. Stick with Step 1 for ten minutes. Longer, if you can take the stares of all your friends who think you've finally flipped out. Unless they have ever missed a class. Then they'll be pulling for you.

Step 2. Walk abjectly into the classroom, up to the teacher's desk, and throw yourself on the floor in front of it. Talk to the floor. Begin by asking its forgiveness. Actually, you are asking the teacher's forgiveness, but practice on the floor first. The teacher will love the fact that you not only *know* that you are scum, but that you also realize that you are just a little bit higher than the dirt in the cracks of the floor. You are despicable. After you have begged forgiveness of the floor (or, as it's known in theological circles, "floor-giveness") for five minutes or so, you may look up slightly in appeal to what grain of human compassion your teacher might have. If you have been convincing, you might hear:

A. You are forgiven;

B. You may have any handouts that you missed; and

C. You should see that smart kid, Marion

Shore, who never misses class, does all his assignments, and will probably grow up to be a successful CPA, and ask if you can borrow some class notes.

One important thing about the second series is that no explanation about why you missed class is necessary. Did you notice that? That's because the teacher doesn't care *why* you missed. This is good because then you don't have to strain you brain coming up with a legitimate-sounding reason. The reason this is good is that you probably don't have one.

All that a teacher cares about is the fact that you missed class. The why is not important. How you intend to make up for it is. Everyone likes to be made to feel that they have power. The latter technique of begging forgiveness does that. You give them power over you. They like that. They glory in the fact that you know your place. They like to see you grovel on the floor! That's because they remember all the times they did that when they were your age. Now it's time to get even.

In spite of the way it seems, missing a class is not the worst thing you'll ever do. Okay, so maybe it is. Try not to do it.

There are times we miss life, too. Sometimes we get so busy doing one thing we forget to go on to the next. Or we think we like doing one thing so much, that we could never like anything else as well. That's our loss. There is so much more to life than what we even imagine.

That's another thing that's neat about this life that God created for us. There's a lot to it. It's not just one-dimensional. There's something in it for everyone. Usually there's a lot for everyone.

Still, some people miss life. Oh, they are around, but they end up missing it just the same. They waste their lives on drugs or drinking. Years go by, and they don't remember a thing—other than that they were high. Or low.

This happens far too often. Some people are lucky and get help. They kick the stuff that has held them captive. And they begin to live again. Sometimes they aren't so lucky. Then they survive, but never live. They don't enjoy life, they merely endure it from one pill, smoke, needle, or drink to the next. They are living, but not really alive.

God wants His children to really live. And we are all God's children, whether we think so or not. He's given us a life to do with what we want. We have the choice. To live or survive. To get high on drugs or high on life. To be controlled or in control.

Think about what is more important to you. What do you want life to be like?

If you miss class, say a little prayer. You'll need it. If you're starting to miss life—say a lot of prayers. Call 1-800-GOD-CARES now.

You'll need it even more

24

DEAR DR. LEAKING:

HOW CAN I LEARN TO TAKE GOOD NOTES?

LAUREL IN LUTESVILLE, MISSOURI

Dear Laurel:
I really would like to answer your question, but I'm afraid you haven't given me enough information. What kind of notes? Are you talking about class notes, musical notes, or love notes?

Since you are the typical American teen, let's begin with the one you're probably most interested in. We'll take the last one first.

Taking Good Love Notes

The secret to taking really good love notes is finding the right boy and girl. You need to determine which couple seems to be most in love in your school. You know the one I mean. They are fairly easy to spot. They look like Siamese twins joined at the hands and lips Their eyes are always locked onto each other's. Their conversation seems to consist mostly of saying their names.

"Oh, Jennifer."

"Oh, Nathaniel!"

"Oh, Jennifer, Jennifer, Jennifer."

"Oh, Naathhaaanniieell."

If you're having difficulty determining the couple that is most in love, go up to one and listen to how they talk to each other. If the conversation is so sweet that it would kill a diabetic, you're warm. If it makes you want to puke, this is the couple you're looking for.

You see, there is something about true love that seems to fry your brain. You know the TV commercial where the guy has a hot skillet and an egg and says, "Watch close. This is your brain; this is your brain on drugs. Any questions?" He could do the same ad substituting the word *love*. People in love are on the most powerful drug ever. Their brains get scrambled or over easy. They say and do the dumbest things. And they aren't even aware of it. People listen to them talk and reach for the barf bag. They don't even notice.

That's love. Makes you want to be in it, doesn't it? But back to the subject at hand. Taking good love notes.

Once you find the right couple, it's easy to take good notes. They will pass them to each other all the time. In class. In study hall. In the cafeteria. In the hall. In the bathroom (I've never figured out how they manage to accomplish that, but they do). In the car on the way home.

Taking notes is a cinch. Remember, these people are legally brain dead. To take the notes, all you have to do is jostle one or the other of them so they drop everything they are carrying. Then be polite and offer to help them pick it all up. Give them back all their books, papers, pencils, and notebooks. Give them back everything but the love notes.

They won't miss them. Chances are they won't even know they are gone. When you get 4,985 love notes a day, who's going to miss one? So you are safe.

Then, being the good person you are, with deep respect for other people's feelings and property, call all your friends over and read them out loud. These notes will be about the funniest things you've ever read. They'll be really gushy and gooey and sappy and stupid. And great help for you when you're in love and need to write notes.

That is how you take really good love notes.

But perhaps those weren't the kind of notes you were thinking about. Maybe you meant musical notes. Let's look at them now.

Taking Good Musical Notes

Before we begin this section, it's time for a little musical humor. Laurel, do you know what the great composer Beethoven is doing today? Why, he's *de-composing*. Oh well, I guess you have to be a music major to appreciate that. Back to taking good musical notes.

The best way to take good musical notes is to get a piece by Bach, Beethoven, or Brahms and photocopy the exact notes they wrote. These guys are generally considered to have written some good stuff, so taking what they composed is a good bet. If you do this you should end up with some pretty good notes. I wouldn't claim them for my own, if I were you. People might recognize them. Even if you did change your name to Carterhooven.

Another way to take good notes is to copy exactly what the teacher puts on the board. I mean exactly. To do that, get some of that funny lined paper. Also have on hand a number 2 pencil. Put every note exactly where it should be and also include such silly-looking things as ♯'s and 𝄞 's. For some reason these are important. If you do it all just as it's on the board you will have taken good notes. If not, you'll have taken bad notes. Which of the two you have done will be evident as soon as you play or sing your notes.

On the off chance that you were not talking about either of the other two, here are some general guidelines for taking good class notes.

Taking Good Class Notes

Get a tape recorder.

In academics it is important to record everything the teacher says. Do not be fooled into asking them what *they* think is important. If you do they will tell you, "Just the important stuff." This sounds easy enough to you. You know what's important. The only problem is that what you consider important (nothing they say) and what they consider important (everything they say) are two different things.

If you took their advice, you would end up with a blank page in your notebook. They, on the other hand, would expect you to have written a book of notes just on that period. Even if you did write a note or two, you can be sure what you wrote wouldn't appear on the upcoming test, while some obscure thing like the year Columbus discovered America (a. 1492, b. 1169, c. 1953) would. And you'd be out of luck.

So tape-record everything. Take the tape to Dictation Class and see if you can talk (con) someone into transcribing it for you. Then read the transcription. Highlight everything. Memorize all 37 pages. This, Laurel, is how you take good notes.

It is important to take good notes in life, too. And the method is similar. All you need to do is look at everything God says about life. Memorize the entire Bible. Take notes at Sunday school and during church. Not *pass* notes, *take* notes. Tests are coming and you need to be prepared.

Okay, so you don't have to do all that. You do need to glance over the material every now and then, though Take a look at everything. It's not as overwhelming as you think, because God is there to help you make sense of it. He'll help you with your notes, and, if you ask, even with the tests.

Life has lots of tests. God's given you great notes. Go for an *A*.

25

DEAR DR. LEAKING:

WHAT SHOULD I KNOW IN ORDER TO USE THE LIBRARY EFFECTIVELY?

SHELLY IN SHELLEY, IDAHO

Dear Shelly:

The first thing you need to know about the library in order to use it effectively is that it is the big room with all the books in it. You may have passed it by a number of times, wondering what it was. Perhaps you thought it was some sort of storage place for books. Well, it's not. It is called a library, and it is there for your use. Just how you can use it will be explained later.

You are not alone in your lack of knowledge about the library. All that many students know about the library is that it's ruled over by some cranky person who is not a teacher. This is true of every school library in the entire free world. And now that the Iron Curtain has been lifted, we will soon find out what school libraries in Russia and

Stuff Your Guidance Counselor

Eastern Europe are like. My guess is that they are just like here

There are certain characteristics every ruler of the library has in common. This is true no matter what gender, race, creed, color, or national origin they are. One is that they are always called "Librarian." The word *Librarian* comes from two Greek words—*Libros* and *Rarian*. *Libros* means "books" and *rarian* means "shut-up." The significance of this title will be apparent shortly.

Another common characteristic is chronology. Age. The librarian always seems to be in the age range of 74 to 113. They are sometimes older, but they're never younger

The final common characteristic is that their entire vocabulary consists of the word *Shhhhh!* You would think that a person who spends all that time around books would know more than one word. But you're wrong. To learn new words a person has to read new words. Have you ever seen a librarian read? Heck, no. He or she is too busy telling you to "Shhhhh!"

So now you know two important things about the library. One is that it is the big room with all the books. Second, it is controlled by the librarian. These two things are the basic building blocks to using the library. However, if you want to use it *effectively* you need to know some other things. Some of them will take work on your part. I know you want to avoid work, but believe me, a little bit of work here will pay big dividends in goofing off later.

The first thing you need to do is find out whether or not you can be excused from study hall to go the library. If you can, you are well on your way to making effective use of the library. Get excused from study hall every chance you can get. Libraries are a lot more fun than study halls.

Think about it. In study hall you have to kill time by staring at the ceiling or actually doing homework. You have to sit in one seat and you can't talk to your friends. In the library you are free to get up and move around and look at the things you want to. You can search for books or magazines or cassette tapes or just walk around pretending to do that. You will still have a hard time getting a good euchre or Monopoly game going, but you can usually visit with your friends if you gather around a book (those are the things with covers and lots of pages in the middle) and talk in low tones while looking serious. In the library, the appearance of doing anything important with a book is what counts.

So which would you rather do—sit in study hall or visit your friends in the nonfiction section of the library?

The second thing you need to do is find out whether the library subscribes to your favorite magazines. Chances are it doesn't. There aren't many school librarians who feel that *Mad, Cracked,* and *Cosmo* are appropriate reading for high schoolers. If the library doesn't have your favorites, does it subscribe to any you could look at without learning something by accident? They all will carry *Time, Newsweek*, and *Teacher's Quarterly*. You wouldn't want to read them. But there may be copies of *Sports Illustrated* or *Seventeen* or something else you'd find acceptable. If you want to know if they stock your kind of mag, just ask the librarian.

I know that's a scary thought. How do you speak to someone who's never said more than "Shhhh!" to you? Well, Shelly, you can communicate with Mr. or Mrs. or

Miss or Ms. Librarian if you learn a simple phrase in "Librar-ese." If you learn to use their language you'll do fine. Below is a sample translation.

"Pardon me, most esteemed librarian, dost thou have issues of the periodical entitled *Seventeen* perched upon any of the myriad stacks contained within these hallowed volume-laden walls?" is Librar-ese for "Say, old person, do youse have some *Seventeen*'s layin' around somewheres?"

A polite inquiry such as this in their native tongue will elicit one of the following two responses. "Shhhh!" or "Yeah, they're on the wall over there marked magazines—and what's all this *periodical* stuff anyway? Who are you trying to impress? Gimme a break!"

So now you know many things which will enable you to make effective use of the library. You know you can get out of study hall and kill the period reading magazines. What more could you want?

Oh, I get it, Shelly, you're one of those serious high schoolers. The ones who actually study. Who get to class on time and edge people out of the way as they try to get in the door so you can get a better seat. You want to know how the library can be used for help with homework.

In that case you need to know one other thing—how to find the books you want. To learn that you have to know how the books are arranged. They do this a little differently in the school library than you do in your room at home. For one thing, they don't arrange them by size, going from tallest to shortest or shortest to tallest. They don't put all the skinny books in one place and all the fat ones someplace else. They don't go by color, arranging books by the spectrum. They don't even do it alphabetically.

No, libraries have come up with a kind of novel method. They arrange their books by subjects. I know this is radical, but it does come in handy when you are dealing with more than five books. The size method may work on top of your dresser at home but falls apart at school.

There are good reasons for this method. One is job security for the librarian. Good old Mr. Newby, the librarian, is the only one who ever seems to be able to figure out the Dewey decimal system—or whatever other system he uses. That means the school administration has to keep him around long after the mandatory retirement age. He's the only one who can find the books.

Another reason is to help you. Let's say you need a book on dinosaurs. If you find out, with or without Mr. Newby's help, where the dinosaur books are you can go to that stack (that's "Librar-ese" for shelves). There you will find all the books on dinosaurs. Except the one you want. Or need.

That's another thing you need to learn about libraries. The book you want will always be checked out already. This will be true your entire academic career. The only way to make sure you and not someone else gets it is to get it first. I know that sounds simple but it's not. It requires some planning and foresight. To accomplish this you have to be the first one there. Ask all your teachers for a list of books they want you to read from now until school's out in June. Then go to the library the day after school starts (waiting one day makes you look not quite so anxious) and check them all out. That's right, get them all. Store them in you locker until you need them. Of course, you may need to rent out other lockers, too.

Which brings us to another thing you need to know. That is what secret method they use to arrange the books by subject matter. What code do they use? How—other than reading the titles off the shelves—do you find where the books you want are? One way to find out is to ask the librarian. Remember what success you had trying to get a magazine. Mr. Newby will be even more helpful here. He will very politely ask you if you have looked in the card catalog first? When you say no, he will beat you about the head and shoulders with a library card and tell you to do that first and quit pestering him.

That takes you to the card catalog. Now, it is important to realize that the card catalog is not a catalog of cards. Don't go over to it expecting to find jacks and aces and kings and queens. There won't be any Rook or Old Maid cards. You won't even find Hallmark cards. So why do they call it a card catalog? Who knows?

The card catalog is a catalog of all the books the library has. To use it you pull out the drawer marked "Da–Do" and look up *Dinosaurs*. Under *Dinosaurs* you will find a listing of all the books they have about dinosaurs. These are listed on little cards (maybe that's why they call it a card catalog) that have the title, author, a short description, and a number like 568.2. What that tells you is to look for the section where all the books numbered 568.2 are and you'll find all the books about dinosaurs.

Those are the essentials you need to know so that you can use the library effectively.

Besides the one at school, you have another library you can use. It is called a Bible. The Bible is more than one book, even though it is all under one cover. It is actually lots of books. And, though it doesn't use the Dewey decimal system, it is arranged by subjects. You have the books of the Law, history, poetry, major prophets, minor prophets, the gospels, the letters, and finally Revelation. Each book has a peculiar and particular point of view. They each have something to teach their readers.

You need to learn to use the Bible effectively. The main thing you need to know to be able to do that is that even though it is many books, it has one main theme. That is how God loves and wants to help His people. Throughout the Bible you will read about how God and humans can work and live and grow together. He does that in the history books. It is expressed in poetry. And the gospels tell the Good News of how God became One of us so that we might live life as it should be lived.

So the next time you are in your school library, think about God's library. It has parts that will bring you comfort and parts that will make you uneasy. Some of it you'll love and lots of it will be hard to take. But ask God, through His Spirit, to help you read through it.

He's one Librarian who won't tell you "Shhhhh!"

26

DEAR DR. LEAKING:

WHAT IS THE DIFFERENCE BETWEEN AN ESSAY EXAM AND AN OBJECTIVE EXAM?

ANNIE IN ANNA, ILLINOIS

Dear Annie:
　The difference between an essay exam and an objective one is like the difference between night and day, black and white, salt and pepper—well, you get the idea. There are a lot of differences. They are not subtle ones either. After reading this chapter you will be able to take one glance at a test and tell if it is an objective test or an essay exam.
　Knowing which is which is important. You see, each has its advantages. Kids in school tend to do better on one type of exam than they do on another. It all depends upon which type of student they are. We'll take a look at which test works best for which student later on. First, though, let's take a look at the differences between an essay exam and an objective one.

The Objective Test

Objective tests generally use one of three types of questions. These are true and false, multiple choice, and short answer. Many objective tests use a mix of these three, chosen in random order. Very rarely will you see a test made up entirely of true and false, multiple choice, or short answer questions. Teachers use a mix to keep you off guard and wondering what kind of question is coming next.

To show how objective questions differ from one another, I have used the same question three times in the examples below. The question is formatted along the lines of one of the three main objective-test styles.

True-or-False Question

Christopher Columbus was from central Ohio.

Multiple Choice Question

Christopher Columbus was from a. Ohio
b. Italy
c. Spain
d. None of the above

Short Answer Question

Christopher Columbus was from _____.

Now we'll look at the essay test.

The Essay Test

An essay test is a lot like a long, drawn-out short answer question from an objective test. In fact, it is exactly like that. Except you have to add information to the ba-

Stuff Your Guidance Counselor

sics. To answer an essay question, you have to rely on your ability for total recall. The following is an example of the same question asked on the objective test, this time as an essay exam.

Essay Question

Please tell what Christopher Columbus's national origin was and what ramifications this had on his setting out to find a westerly trade route to India. Check with the teacher if you need additional paper or pencils.

The difference between essay and objective tests should by now be obvious. If it isn't, please place this book face down and repeat the following line—"No, Mr. Jones, sir, I never did graduate from high school, but I still think I could do a really good job collecting trash here at Burger World."

One more time. An essay exam is one where you supply all of the answers and an objective one gives you help. On an objective test, you generally have at least part of the answer in front of you. While this would seem to be an advantage, it can really mess you up. It can play games with your mind. That's because after you look at a question for more than ten seconds *all* of the answers look like they could be right. And only one of them is. How do you figure it out?

When I was in school, I always used my mental faculties to their fullest during a stressful time such as this. How did I determine the right answer? I used "The Tie Breaker." You know, the "eenie, meenie, minie, moe" routine. It works on most any question except a short answer one. For those I just wrote down the first word that bopped into my mind. Well, sometimes I couldn't use the first word.

An essay test, on the other hand, gives you the flexibility to ramble on about anything you think may pertain to the question, up to and including history, art, science, literature, your own personal observations, what you think your mom or dad or cat feels about this subject, whether it applies to today's life-styles and.   . Get the idea? You look at the question and start writing. Go with the flow. Even if you get it all wrong you may win some points for creativity

Each test has its advantages and disadvantages. If you sometimes need a nudge in the right direction, objective tests are for you. After all, there's a little bit of the answer staring you in the face. If you have studied hard, or at least glanced over the work, you should be able to figure out which one is the answer.

Essay exams appeal to those of us who like to approach something from lots of different angles. It is a chance to see for ourselves whether or not we really understand the many facets of the subject we're studying. It is also a chance for us to express ourselves.

Tests, be they objective or essay, aren't much fun. We're under a lot of pressure when we take a test. Our grades, and sometimes our freedom, rides on how well we do. In spite of that, tests are good. They help us determine whether we are just killing time in class or really learning something. Has the time been wasted, or are we going to leave with some actual knowledge tucked under our baseball caps? Tests tell us what we know. And pointedly show us what we don't.

There are tests outside of class, too. Sometimes they are objective and other times they're essay. Like in school, it is easy to tell which is which.

> It's good to take drugs.   T or F

That one's fairly simple. We *know* the right answer Whether we live it or not is something else.

> It is okay to lie.   a. never
>   b. sometimes
>   c. if no one gets hurt
>   d. none of the above

That one's harder. What did you put for an answer? Then you will have essay exams.

> "Jo, how do you feel about having sex with someone before you're married? Why?"

You can be sure that you are going to have lots of exams thrown at you. Life is a tough teacher. Getting a passing grade, even a $C-$ is not always easy. The important thing is to have studied so that you can face the unexpected exams and answer the way you want to.

If you want some help studying, ask Jesus. He's always there and wants you to get a passing grade. Just knowing that He's there can sometimes be all you need when you face some of life's difficult tests. He can help you through them.

Taking life's tests with Jesus' help is a lot like being able to take an algebra test with all your notes, books, and the teacher whispering the processes in your ear. With help like that you'd be sure to pass.

With Jesus walking beside you, you'll be sure to pass all of life's tests, too. Just learn to walk close to Him and listen real carefully.

27

DEAR DR. LEAKING:
WHAT IS PASS/FAIL?
JONATHON IN JUAB, UTAH

Dear Jonathon:

Pass/Fail is when a quarterback takes the snap from center, drops back, throws to one of the eligible receivers, and the pass is (a) dropped or (b) intercepted. The pass has failed, thereby acquiring the designation "Pass/Fail."

Now on the off chance that this is not the pass/fail you were referring to, let us look at another form of pass/fail. The academic pass/fail.

A class that is referred to as pass/fail is different from other classes. It is not different because you can pass or fail in it. As you are well aware, you can pass or fail in any class. I don't know of any class you can't fail in. I know some I could never pass, but I never was in a class I couldn't flunk.

What makes a pass/fail class different from a regular pass-it-or-fail-it class is that you don't get a grade. The school administration should call it No/Grade, not pass/fail. This is one class you cannot, no matter how hard you try, get a *D–* in. That's good. It won't pull your grade point average down any lower than it is now. Of course, you can't get an *A* either. But then that's probably not too big a problem for you anyhow, is it?

Pass/fail classes come in real handy for those of you who have older siblings. That's school-psychologist talk for big brothers or sisters. If you do have older siblings, chances are you have taken (or are going to take) some of the same classes they took when they were in high school. You may even have some of the same teachers. This is generally not to your benefit.

Let's say your older sister, Whitney, is a really smart kid. Okay, there's no chance of that in your mind, but somehow she's got the school fooled. She's popular with the teachers and gets good grades. This is bad news for you.

Every time you take a class that she took, you will be held up for comparison. And found wanting.

"Well, I *never* had trouble like that from Whitney," sighs Mrs. Pfenninger.

"Whitney *never* forgot to do her homework," exclaims Mr. McGrew.

"Whitney got all *A*'s in my class," says Miss Hannon. "What seems to be *your* problem?"

Whitney's a pain in the rear, thinks you.

Which is true. She is to you. The only way you can win with an older sibling who went to the same school is if he flunked every class, including remedial remedial, burned the school to the ground, and was shipped off to reform school. If he did all that, you would have a chance to look better. To the teachers. The kids would all like your brother better.

Pass/fail helps you here. You see, by taking a pass/fail you don't have to worry about your parents ragging you about your grade in that class. What can they say? "Try harder. Your sister Whitney got a pass." No, they can't say that. It sounds too stupid, even for parents, who are known for saying stupid things. They *can* urge you not to fail. And trust me, you better not. If you did, you'd be the first kid ever to fail a pass/fail.

You see, pass/fail was created by some sympathetic school administrator. I know you think there aren't any. There aren't many. But there was one somewhere who remembered the trauma of sibling school rivalry. He or she came up with the idea of pass/fail. Central to the concept is that the classes had to be impossible to fail. The reasoning was that it's bad enough to get an *F* in regular class. It would be emotionally and mentally devastating to fail a class that had no grades. No one could ever live that down. So while there may be classes that are easier than pass/fail classes ... nah, there just aren't any.

So, good news. There are some classes even *you* can pass without breaking a sweat—or cracking a book.

You do have to be a little careful, though. Some wily teacher types have actually crafted pass/fail classes that are challenging. I know that this goes against the original intent of the creator. (No, not God. The creator of the pass/fail concept.) But you know how unscrupulous teachers are. Be careful what kind of pass/fail you sign up for.

Of course, even the difficult pass/fail classes give you a lot of options. Just how many options depends on how many different kinds of classes your school offers. With pass/fail you can try anything. You can try things you know you would never ace without having to worry about them pulling your grade point average down. You can register for some subject you always thought would be interesting but didn't want to risk getting a *D* in. You can be an academic adventurer.

"Indiana Bud and the Search for the Effects of Styrofoam on the Environment! Coming soon to a classroom near you!!"

So pass/fail saves you from siblings and opens new horizons fairly painlessly. What more could you ask from a class? Well, okay, knowing you, you could ask a lot more. But you've got to admit, pass/fail is a pretty good deal with very little risk.

Life has its share of pass/fail, too. As a matter of fact, it's all pass/fail. That's the way God set it up. No one is going to get *A*'s or 100s on life. The Bible tells us that everyone falls short. As if you needed the Bible to tell you that. You have seen people you know, and maybe even look up to, fail. They've let you or someone else down. That happens. It's part of life. It's not that people want to get *D*'s in life instead of *A*'s. It's just that life is too tough to 4.0. Only one Person has ever managed to do that.

That Person is Jesus. He got all *A*'s. But it wasn't easy. He's on our side now. And pass/fail is in effect for all of life. To pass you have to want to walk close to Jesus' side and imitate His life. You won't get it right all the time. The important thing is to try. With Him, that's all that matters—that you love God and walk with Jesus.

When you walk with God, you'll learn lots of new things. You'll have your horizons stretched. You can live more confidently knowing that the old grading scale has been put away for good. Jesus likes pass/fail. Actually,

He likes pass. He hates fail. That's why He made it so easy.

Ask Jesus to walk with you. Follow Him as closely as you can. Realize that you won't pass every test. Just keep on walking. Keep on studying. Try to live as He wants you to. That way you'll pass. And that's all that matters.

28

DEAR DOCTOR LEAKING:

IF IT COMES AT THE VERY END OF HIGH SCHOOL, WHY DO THEY CALL IT COMMENCEMENT?

KIM IN KAUNAKAKAI, HAWAII

Dear Kim:
This is not an unusual question. Students throughout the ages have asked this same question. So have many teachers, school administrators, and parents. Now, they will not admit that they are confused. That's forbidden by the rules that govern being an adult. Instead they will mumble a lot and say something similar to,

> "Well, Kim, my boy, the reason it is called commencement is because, now, even though you are finishing your high school career, you are getting ready to go out into the world. You are 'commencing' a new life, you are beginning

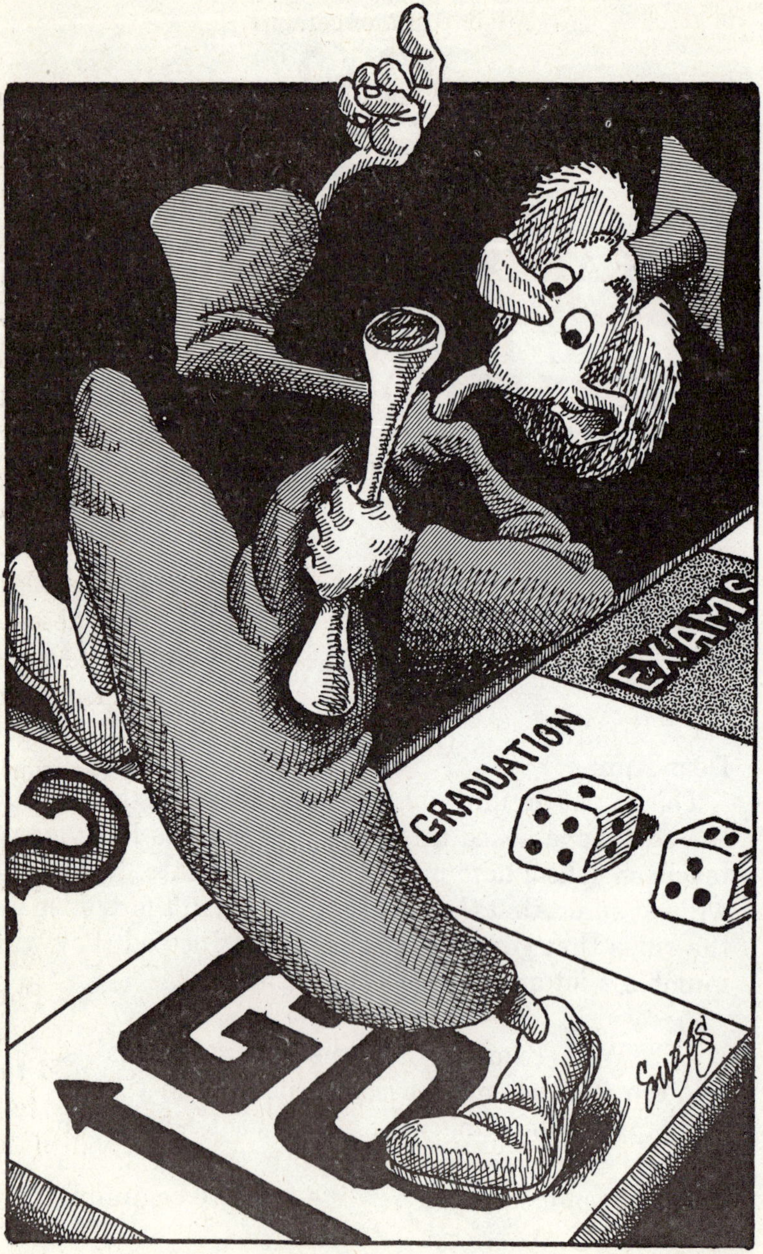
EXAMS
GRADUATION
GO

> on a new path—the path of adulthood. That's why it's called 'commencement.'"

You probably don't buy that any more than *they* did when their parents told it to them. It's too pat, too simple to be believable. So what is the answer? What is the question? Oh yes, why do they call it commencement if it's at the end?

To really understand this, we need to look at the word and where it came from. The root origin of the word *commencement* has been shrouded in mystery for years. Only after exhaustively poring over the dictionary for minutes on end was I able to uncover from whence *commencement* came. It came—from the dictionary. But even before the dictionary it was derived from two ancient Egyptian words. I realize that this is startling. Very few of our modern English words descend from the Egyptian language. This is probably because very few of us descend from the Egyptian people. The story of how this fact was discovered is one of the more amazing in archaeological word digs.

Our story begins in 1935, halfway around the world (unless of course you are reading this in Cairo). It all began with two explorers who found the vast, previously undiscovered pyramid of the great Egyptian Pharaoh Domino's pizza (May 19, 1689 B.C. to January 4, 1632 B.C.). Little is known about his reign because it lasted 30 minutes or less and they got three decades off their next Pharaoh.

At any rate, these two explorers who discovered the previously undiscovered—sorry, I forgot I said that, let's move on—found amazing hieroglyphics on the wall of the pyramid. They seemed to show a sort of outstanding scene of a primitive rite wherein thousands of Egyptian young people were standing around wearing black robes and flat pieces of cardboard on their heads while being lectured to by very boring adults. The next scene was one of great partying. The scene that followed that was of the young people sacking foodstuffs at some sort of depository for consumables or sitting in high chairs watching people mass bathe. The final scene was one of adult males cheering and adult females crying as all the worldly possessions of the young Egyptians were piled into chariots in preparation of going to a far distant land called Stateuniversity—the only Egyptian word that was decipherable.

The two explorers pondered and pondered this depiction. What was this rite? What did it mean? They pondered and pondered until, at their wits end (which is where they were sitting), they opened the sarcophagus of the dead Pharaoh. When they swept away the dust of the millennia they saw the answer clasped in the corpse's hand. So you could say, their mummy told them.

What their mummy told them was this, "Kummenz Mhet." Which is early Egyptian for "Get out of high school and get on with living."

That is why it is known as commencement. It has nothing to do with the modern English interpretation. It is all about getting on with life.

Though high school graduation is a big one, there are lots of commencements in life. When you commence to drive, when you commence to date, when you commence to clean up your room without being told to. Life is full of beginnings. And endings.

Never Told You

Your time in school is ending. You may never again see some of the people you've spent four years with. No more Mullenville High. No more harassment in the hallways. Life, as you have known it, is ending. A new life is waiting for you to begin it.

There is always one constant. God. The Bible says He is the *alpha* and the *omega*. That's Greek for beginning and end. What it means in Sunday school is that God is the beginning and ending to everything. Without Him, time, the world, and everything else would never have started.

What it means on a day-to-day basis to you is that God will be with you at every beginning and ending you have.

29

DEAR DR. LEAKING:

WHAT COMES AFTER HIGH SCHOOL?

STAN IN SOAP LAKE, WASHINGTON

Dear Stan:
What comes after high school? There's a wide range of things that can come. It all depends upon what you want to come. What things have you dreamed about? You'll find you can become what you dream. How many times have you dreamed the following?

> He could hear his mother softly sobbing, see his little brothers' and sisters' faces pressed against the glass of the living room window as his father, voice choked with emotion, patted him on the back and said, "Make us proud, son." *As if there were any doubt of that,* he thought to himself. The autumn sun streamed through the trees on the front lawn, casting shifting patterns on the freshly mown grass. He had mowed

it for the last time. One of his little brothers would mow it now. He was a man, on his own. Heading for the car loaded with all his belongings, he tossed off a wave to his kid sister, blew a kiss to his mom, ready at last for college.

And leaving the small town behind, he—

BRRRRIIINNNNGGGGG!!!!

How many times during your senior year of high school was your life interrupted by the bell. You sat looking out the window, dreaming of how it would feel to finally be free, no more Mom or Dad to tell you what to do, no more sharing rooms with stupid siblings, able to stay up as late and sleep as late as you want. Free to do what you want, when you want.

A recent study by the Leaking-Fawcett Center for Recent Studies, showed that the average teenager spends around eight hours a day dreaming this dream, or a variation on it.

Chances are you, Stan, are one of those teenagers. You have probably spent more time thinking and dreaming about college this last year than preparing for it. It looms before you; it is about to quit being a dream and become reality.

High school will soon be over. Graduation will be nothing more than a Kodacolor memory of mortarboards sailing through a summer evening. Fall will be here before you know it. And with autumn comes leaving for school. Not going back. *Leaving*. Going away. Far from hearth and home, hopefully.

All of your life you have been preparing for this

moment—adulthood. You have taken the right courses, learned your lessons, gotten good (at least passing) grades, and graduated. Now it's up to you.

Life is lying before you, no matter what choices you've made. You may be going to college or tech school. You might be getting a job. Whatever happens next depends on you. Whatever you have dreamed is here.

What is going to happen after high school? I can't tell you. It's not that I don't want to, I just can't. The only thing I can tell you is that it's up to you to make what you have dreamed of come true. You are on your own.

Well, not completely. Your folks and friends are still there. But not in quite the same way they were before. The choices you make will largely be left up to you. And so will the joys or sorrows of those choices. You have to learn to choose wisely.

God is there for you, as well. But, like your parents or friends, He won't make the choices for you. Part of God's plan is that we all learn to live ourselves. We aren't locked into some sort of machinelike life, where we do what we were programmed to do. God has given us the freedom to do with our lives what we want, with or without help from Him.

With help from Him is the better of the two. It's rough being on your own. I know you may not believe that. Right now, being on your own sounds like heaven. But it can be tough. Scary. Lonely. Making decisions is not always easy. How can you know whether or not you made the right one? What if you have really goofed something up? And not just a homework assignment that you'll have a chance to correct, either.

You do need to remember that God is there. He's been

with you and for you through high school. He will be with you and for you after high school, too. God will walk with you all of your life. Sometimes He may walk so quietly you don't even know He's there. But He is. All you have to do is slow down sometimes and look for Him. It won't really be much of a search.

What comes after high school? I'm afraid I don't know. But I can tell you *who* comes after high school.

God does.

30

DEAR DR. LEAKING:

NOW THAT I AM ON MY OWN, HOW DO I FIND AN APARTMENT?

BROOKS IN BARDSTOWN, KENTUCKY

Dear Brooks:

Finding an apartment is not that hard. All you have to do is look for something that looks like a big house. A really big house. A *huge* house. A house that ate lots of other, littler houses. Something that is to houses what King Kong is to Cheetah. After you find such a place and determine that it is not an office building (i.e., a building full of offices), then most probably it is an apartment building (i.e., a building full of apartments).

In spite of the elegant and simple phrasing of your question, something about it tells me that you are asking more than just how to find an apartment. I get the strange feeling that what you want to know, Brooks, is how to acquire an apartment of your very own. A place where you can install your long-dreamed-of killer stereo and hang your Rocky the Flying Squirrel matching towels in the bathroom. Isn't that right?

That is much tougher. Not everyone wants someone with a killer stereo in their apartment. Most people will put up with the cartoon towels, but 950 watts shooting out of 12 floor-to-ceiling speakers is not always welcome. Especially by the little old lady living downstairs who has a hard time getting her door to close tight. So plan on taking some quality time if you really want to find the place that is just right for you. Or even a place that will have you.

Getting your own apartment is important. Especially your first one. It is one of the mile-markers along your freeway to adulthood. You are no longer going to be living with Mommy and Daddy. You are declaring your independence. Which is nothing you haven't been doing since you were about two. This time, though, as you set out to find your apartment, you are not only declaring it—you are staking it out. You want your apartment to reflect your newfound freedom. You want it to make a statement about who you are and what you are like. So you go in search of the perfect place.

Finding it doesn't seem like it should be that hard. Trust me, it is. Yes, there are pages of ads for apartments in the paper and on TV. There are thousands of them advertised daily. These ads all show apartments that are "affordable with all the amenities." This sounds like a good combination. *It's just what I've been looking for,* you think, *affordable with all the amenities.* And that's a big mistake. Being a high school graduate you assume you know what *affordable* and *amenities* mean. You don't.

Sure, you may have a rudimentary grasp on the con-

Stuff Your Guidance Counselor

cepts these two words embody. You may even be able to use them in a sentence that makes sense. But you know how to use them in conversation—not advertising. And there is a big difference. You see, in advertising there are many definitions for these two words. Two of them are on opposite ends of the continuum—your definition and the apartment manager's. Let's look at this more closely.

First, affordable. This sounds simple enough. Affordable means you can afford it. True, you are on your first job or starting college. Your funds are limited. You need a place to stay that will fit within your budget. So you look for all the ads that have the word *affordable* in them. If it says *affordable,* you assume it means affordable to you. You think it means that if you have income from work, grants, parents, or bank robbery amounting to $1,000.00 a month, about $24.95 should go to rent. That would be *affordable*—and leave enough for other important things like food, movies, concerts, and a new car. Yes, $24.95 is a nice number when you think about rent.

It seems so to the leasing company, too. The only difference is you mean $24.95 a month and they mean $24.95 a day. To them *affordable* is whatever outrageous price they can afford to charge. In addition, their ads are written by some $53,000-a-year copywriter at the ad agency who thinks $24.95 a day is affordable since it is to her.

Some apartment leasing firms do have a heart. Since you are just starting out, they may give you a break and lower the rent from $24.95 a day. If you are lucky enough to find such a place, after you pay your rent they may leave you about $24.95 a month for extras like movies, concerts, bus fare, and food.

Amenities has different meanings, too. To you *amenties* means a heated, olympic-size pool, a Jacuzzi in your bathroom, lighted tennis and basketball courts, gas barbecue grills, a tanning booth, weight room, a championship golf course, and water-skiing on the lake at "Lakefront Apartments." That doesn't seem unreasonable. In fact, after looking at the ads in the paper, you think you may have set your expectations too low. You haven't.

You see, to the owners of the apartment complex, *amenities* takes on a whole new meaning. To them it means you will have a roof that usually doesn't leak and indoor plumbing that doesn't either. As far as water-skiing on the lake—well, if you can get going fast enough to get up on a quarter acre of algae-infested pond scum, you're welcome to ski.

It is easy to get burned renting your first apartment. You are so excited about having a place of your own that you are willing to overlook the little things like having no stove or refrigerator, or glass in the windows, and paper-thin walls. Of course, if you don't have any money left over after rent you really don't need a stove or refrigerator because you don't have any food to heat or refrigerate. And the paper-thin walls may provide all the entertainment you can afford.

Before you even begin to look for an apartment, though, you need to decide whether to get a furnished or unfurnished apartment. The major part of this decision will be predicated on whether you have furniture or not.

At this stage of life, your choice in furniture will probably come down to whatever is hiding in your folks' attic

Stuff Your Guidance Counselor

or whatever is on sale at Goodwill. This is not a tough call.

The stuff your parents want you to take is stuff they bought when they were young married people and thought they had taste. So they bought lamps with dancing gypsies on them, blond furniture, and faked oil paintings. These they are willing to give to you. This seems terribly generous of them. And it is—with the emphasis on terribly. Why would you want this stuff? Your parents don't. They haven't since 1963. They know it's hideous. If they didn't, why else would it all be hidden away so no one can see it? And now they want to give it to you. No thanks!

Goodwill is a better bet because nobody, not even your folks, gives really tacky, tasteless stuff to them. After all, Goodwill comes and picks it up at your house. Your folks don't want the guys collecting for Goodwill to know how bad their taste was when they first got married. And they are certainly not going to risk having some nosy neighbor get a peek at it. So if you have no furniture, and you really want some, buy Goodwill.

If you don't really want to mess with Goodwill or hand-me-downs from the nightmare of bad taste, renting a furnished apartment may seem like the best idea. It's not. Furnished apartments are generally furnished one of two ways. If it's a privately owned apartment, it's the cast-off, tacky furniture of the owner. They just stuck it in the apartment they're trying to rent instead of carrying it up to the attic.

If it's in an apartment complex, you can bet the furniture was sold to them by the same guy who sold your folks all that stuff that is now hiding in their attic. And you know what kind of taste that guy has. If the apartment doesn't have new tacky stuff with blond wood and lots of formica, then it's furniture that is made out of two-by-fours and plywood. The apartment owners put that kind in because that way it won't matter if you destroy it.

My advice is to go with an unfurnished apartment and shop at Goodwill. Or Waterbeds 'R' Us. After all, you spend one-third of your life in bed. In your case this will probably be daytime hours, as nights are far too valuable to waste sleeping. Besides there's nothing quite as exciting as going to sleep on a water bed with a leak. Especially to the guy in the apartment below you.

Finding an apartment is exciting and scary. You have to learn to deal with the electric company, the gas company, the phone company, pay your own bills, read the fine print in the lease, and so on. Each place seems to require a deposit and has all kinds of rules and regulations. If you haven't discovered it by now, it is here you will find out that the freedom of being an adult is a myth.

Having an apartment means you are on your own. It is yours—whether it is a three-bedroom townhouse in the Golden Ghetto or someone's former garage, featuring an oil stain the size of Columbus, Ohio, in the middle of your "spacious living-dining area." It may not be much, but it is yours.

There is one Person you should invite over for an apartment-warming right away. That's God. God wants to share your new place with you. And even if you are on your own, you may find that you would still like some company. God is a Guest who never comes unless invited.

Of course, He'll stay till He's told to leave, but that's a chance worth taking.

One thing you will find out as you go through life is that God can go with you—and will—wherever you go. If you want Him to, that is. He can be the unseen Guest at every meal. He can be there on the first lonely nights sitting on cast-off furniture. Make sure God is there with you. After all, His home has always been your home. Return the favor. Make your home His home. Make Him welcome there. You will never find a better roommate. Or a quieter one.

31

DEAR DR. LEAKING:

HOW DO I BALANCE MY CHECKBOOK?

TINA IN TRUTH OR CONSEQUENCES, NEW MEXICO

Dear Tina:
  Balancing a checkbook is not nearly as difficult as it sounds. I have found that the best way to balance a checkbook is to take the checkbook, place it horizontally on my middle finger while my hand is palm up with the first finger pointing at the ceiling, and then hold very still. If I have taken my time and mentally prepared myself, I can usually balance a checkbook this way for quite a while. I'll bet you can learn to do it, too.
  If by some chance this is not the sort of checkbook balancing you had in mind, then further examination of the subject might be in order. You might be thinking of the financial aspects and dimensions of modern banking and high finance as it relates to your overall cash flow, debits and credits, and subsidiary activities. In other words, how much money you've got.

Stuff Your Guidance Counselor

Besides your own apartment, one of the most important tools of independence is your checkbook. Getting a checkbook is relatively simple. All you have to do is go down to your local bank and give Mr. Johnston, the bank president, some money. By some money I am talking more in the neighborhood of a couple *hundred* dollars than just a couple dollars. Mr. Johnston does not get very excited about someone trying to open a checking account with two dollars. Well, actually, he does get very excited, but it's not the kind of excitement you want.

After you have given Mr. Johnston your money, he will give you a little book with lots of numbered pieces of paper in it. All blank. At first glance this does not seem to be an equitable exchange. At second glance it doesn't either. But learn to trust your banker. You can, you know. That's why they are called trust officers. What at first and second glance seems to be a raw deal, is in fact good news. Mr. Johnston has just given you a checkbook. Now anytime you want to use any of the money you gave him, you simply take one of those numbered, blank pieces of paper, write the amount you want to use, who you want to give the money to, and your name, and you have written a check. It's as good as money. Almost.

Why the almost? That's because a check is as good as money only if you remember one simple rule: You must have given (or continue to give) Mr. Johnston enough money to equal the amount of checks you have written. Just giving him money once is not enough. Unless of course there were about 20 zeros between the first number and decimal point marking cents. You probably are not in a position to hand Mr. Johnston

$500,000,000,000,000,000,000, so some further explanation is probably in order.

You see, Tina, there are two frequent errors people have concerning checking accounts. One is, "I can't be overdrawn, I still have checks in the checkbook." While this sounds logical—the number of checks should somehow equal the number of dollars available for use—it doesn't work that way. Just because you have checks left doesn't mean you still have money left to spend. Remember our simple rule: Keep giving Mr. Johnston money. It is very important to follow that rule. Let's look at an example.

Let's say you have written a $1,000 check to Old Man Polivick in payment for his gas-guzzling old Cadillac with the nifty 8-track tape player. You have driven the car home (stopping at every service station along the three-mile route between his house and yours), and he is heading for the bank to cash your check. You better have already given Mr. Johnston $1,000 to cover your check. Better yet, you better have given Mr. Johnston $1,001. (I forgot to tell you he also makes you pay for the privilege of using your money each time you write a check. But more about that later.)

It is important to have given Mr. Johnston $1,001 for two reasons. One is that when Old Man Polivick comes in to cash your check, the bank people will look to see how much you have given Mr. Johnston. If it doesn't add up to $1,000 they won't give Old Man Polivick his $1,000 *and* they will charge *you* $10 or $20 for writing a bad check. The second reason is that Old Man Polivick will not be a happy camper and will come over to

Stuff Your Guidance Counselor

your house and, even though he's old and short and funny-looking, pound you so low into the ground that you will have to reach up to tie your Reeboks. And he'll take his Cadillac home with him. That's if he is in a good mood.

If he's not (and Old Man Polivick hardly ever is), he'll call the police and *they* will come over, take his Cadillac back, and give you a free ride to jail for writing a bad check.

Can you say, "Writing bad checks is illegal?"

Read your county court news and you'll see how many people in your town learned to say that last week.

Can you say, "Go directly to jail and don't pass go?"

Many of them learned that, too.

The other error people make is assuming that the bank will balance their checkbook for them. They have somehow gotten the mistaken impression that since they gave their money to Mr. Johnston, he will keep tabs on it for them and let them know when they are about to come up short.

Wrong. Mr. Johnston has more to do than keep track of your checkbook for you. He's a banker, for goodness sakes, not some petty clerk. He's got important, banking type things to do. Like go golfing if it's summer or skiing when the snow flies and the powder's fresh. How's he supposed to do important banking duties like that and keep your checkbook balanced, too?

What Mr. Johnston *will* do (and be grateful for that) is send you a monthly listing of all of your deposits and all of the checks you have written that have been turned into the bank for payment It will also list "service charges." These are the aforementioned charges the bank makes you pay in return for them letting you use your money.

This sounds like a pretty good racket, doesn't it? It is kind of like you saying, "John, you give me ten dollars and then when you are ready to use it you can. Of course, you'll have to give me a one dollar handling fee."

If you did that to a few of your friends they would call you pond scum. If you did that to an entire town they would call you a bank.

What the bank statement (that's what the bank calls the previously mentioned listing) tells you is how much money the bank says you have left in your checking account after they have added all your deposits and subtracted your checks and service charges. That's why you need to keep a balanced checkbook, to make sure that you and the bank agree. If you and the bank don't agree, you perform the following simple procedure:

You change your figures to match the bank's.

After all, there's no way the bank could make a mistake. At least no way you'll ever be smart enough to figure out.

So how *do* you balance a checkbook? It is very simple. You add your deposits and subtract your checks. Make it look like the example on the next page.

Stuff Your Guidance Counselor

NUMBER	DATE	CHECKS ISSUED TO OR DESCRIPTION OF DEPOSIT	(−) AMOUNT OF CHECK	√T	(−) CHECK FEE (IF ANY)	(+) AMOUNT OF DEPOSIT	BALANCE 1,234 56
267	5/11	TO/FOR Lakeview Apartments — RENT	450 00				450 00 / 784 56
268	5/11	TO/FOR Paducah Power & Light — ELECTRICITY	94 35				94 35 / 690 21
269	5/12	TO/FOR CD's R Us — CD's	114 20				114 20 / 576 01
270	5/13	TO/FOR Shoes Unlimited — SHOES	498 00				498 00 / 78 01
271	5/15	TO/FOR The House of T-Shirts — SHORTS	70 00				70 00 / 8 01
272	5/15	TO/FOR Arnett's IGA — FOOD FOR THE MONTH	7 30				7 30 / 71

Do this every time you write a check and you will always know how much money, if any, you have left.

Having your own checkbook is another one of those steps on the road to adulthood. It makes you feel good to flip open your checkbook and see the checks all lying there, with your name and address on them, just waiting to do your financial bidding. And they will, as long as your account balance equals your checks written.

There is only one account I know of where you don't have to worry about being overdrawn. That's at the Bank of God. God has come up with a rather unique banking concept, one that probably won't catch on at BankOne or Citicorp.

At the Bank of God every check you write will be covered. Every debit will be paid. This will be done no matter whether you have made a deposit in your account lately or not. You see, once you open an account and make your initial deposit, everything else is taken care of. God takes care of everything. He calls it His "Grace" account.

Your initial deposit is high, though. It requires that you deposit your life. That's costly. It means you'd better be serious as you look into opening this account. After that initial deposit, though, God will do the rest. He will keep your account balance current. In fact, He has already paid everything for you.

So the next time you're dropping off some cash with Mr. Johnston, think of the Bank of God. You might want to check out your account there, make sure it's still open, and God's got your current address. And remember, while BankOne may have 18,000 people who care, God is the only One you really need. That's something you can bank on.

32

DEAR DR. LEAKING:

WHAT HAPPENS IF I GET SICK?

MARINA IN MARIGOLD, MISSISSIPPI

Dear Marina:
  Most of the time what happens is that you feel hot and sweaty or cold, clammy, or chilled and achy, real yucky like you are going to die and you run to the bathroom and throw up. I'm surprised you don't know this at your age. Very few of us ever get to be as old as you are without being sick.
  I suppose there is a chance that there's more to your question than appears on the surface. You may already know what the physical part of being ill is like. Maybe, just maybe, you are asking what is going to happen now that you are on your own. "What," you are asking, "will it be like to be sick now that I don't live at home and Mommy's not there to take care of me?"
  That depends on where you are.
  If you are at college, hardly anything else will happen. You will probably miss classes and tests and throw up in

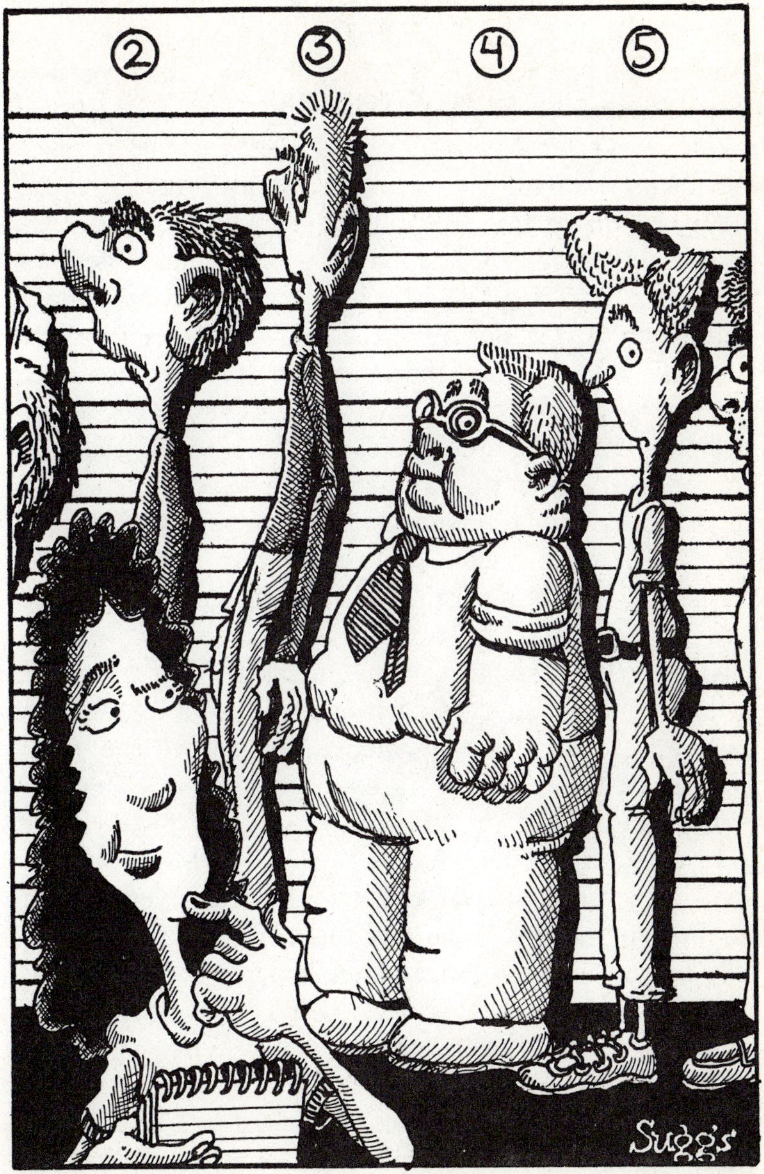
2
3
4
5
Suggs

the dorm bathroom. Even though the college catalog tells you that there is medical staff on duty at all times, it doesn't tell you that Dr. Paparello, the school doctor, doesn't make "room" calls. The only place he calls on regularly is the racquetball court at the Y. If you get sick at college, you're on your own, unless you have a sympathetic roommate. If you do, he or she will bring you crackers from the cafeteria and may even tell your professors you are not missing class due to lack of interest for a change, but you're not there because you are really ill. If you have a very sympathetic roommate, he or she may even transport you to the college clinic where you can sit for hours with other really sick students, waiting for Dr. Paparello to return from his workout. When he gets back he will take your temperature, look at your throat, and say, "Yes, you are sick, go back to your room and get some rest. Nurse McCraine, get this poor student some aspirin and me a court time for tomorrow."

Neither Dr. Paparello nor the college will call your parents and tell them you are sick. Unless of course, you have missed a tuition payment. If you have they will even drive you home. And leave you there.

If, on the other hand, you didn't go to college but rather have taken a job, then you will miss work, paychecks, and throw up in your apartment. Hopefully you will do this in the vicinity of the bathroom. You will also probably lie on the sofa and watch hours of daytime TV, stuff like "The Price Is Right" and "One Day at a Time" reruns. This is okay with your employer. He or she has a hidden motive in allowing you to lie on your sofa with the Sony on. Very few people know who the real sponsors of these shows are. Most people think that the companies whose products are featured in commercials sponsor daytime TV. Not true. Daytime TV is sponsored by the Chamber of Commerce and the local businesses and industries in your town. In other words—your boss.

They do this because they figure if you watch enough daytime TV you will be ready to go back to work since the shows are so bad. There's only so much of Ann Romano and Schneider you can take. How many times can you hear J.J. say, "Dyn-O-Mite!"? Can you put up with even one more time? No way. You may be sick, but you're not brain dead. You'd rather be at work than subjected to "Commmee on dowwwnn!" again.

If you are in the armed services, what branch you serve in determines what will happen. In the navy you'll heave in the head, in the army you will barf in your barracks, in the air force you'll toss your cookies on base, and in the marines you'll puke in your helmet. There's no room for sissies in the marines. Just because you're sick doesn't mean you'll get out of crawling 900 miles through the mud to keep your sergeant happy.

If your parents live close by to you, then Mom may come by and take care of her "little baby." Then again, she may figure that 18 or 19 years of doing that dirty work is enough and leave you on your own. Believe it or not, while moms may like runny eggs, burnt toast, and the heel in the loaf of bread, they really don't care for cleaning up vomit.

And we all know that it is Mom who has always cleaned up after you. Dad doesn't. Fathers seem to have an innate sense that tells them when a kid is about to puke. This sense warns them so they can disappear whenever Mt. Kid is about to erupt. They hear this inner warning and head for their workshop—even though they haven't made anything for years.

Fathers also seem to sense when the mess has been managed and know it is safe to come back up from the basement. "Oh, Neenah, you threw up. Gee, I'm sorry I wasn't here to help you clean yourself up. Good thing Mom was around." Yeah, right. Lucky Mom.

Of course, it is a good thing that fathers have this sense. What happens whenever your father's sense is out of whack and he happens to be around when you or little sister throw up? He pukes, too. It's kind of an esophageal chain reaction. Fathers can't help it. They see someone vomit and they vomit.

So don't count on Mom. She's been counting the days since the day after the day you were born (you *were* really cute for about 24 hours) until you would be on your own. So, clean up your own messes, Mom's got tennis to play, books to read, malls to shop. She may feel bad about not helping at first, but she'll get over it.

About the only Person you can count on when you are sick is God. He says He will never leave or forsake you. Saint Paul (no, not your older brother, even though your parents seem to think he's a saint compared to you) says that nothing can separate us from the love of God. Though Paul doesn't specifically mention barfing, knowing about God's love, I think it's included.

God has seen you when you are good and healthy and when you are good and sick. Or bad and sick. He loves you no matter how you are. He has sympathy pains along with you. He wants you to feel better—inside and out. And when everyone else has left, or is too busy to come over and help, God will be sitting right beside your bed, holding your hand until you feel better.

Sickness is something that happens to us. Too bad it does, but it is a fact of life. A sad fact. God's love is something that happens to us, too. That is a fact of life, as well. A happy fact. God has promised to stand by us through poverty and wealth, sickness and health. That sounds sort of like the vows at a wedding, doesn't it? Which brings us to our next question.

33

DEAR DR. LEAKING:

HOW DO I FIND MR. RIGHT?

JUANITA FROM JUANITA, WASHINGTON

Dear Juanita:

I think the easiest way for you to find Mr. Wright is to look in the phone book. Just turn to the W's. Finding him should not be that difficult if you do that. The only hard part will be knowing which Mr. Wright is the one you want. Is it the one who works at the bank or the one who lives on Hawthorne Drive? Even our little county phone book has over 25 Mr. Wrights. How do you know which one is the right Mr. Wright?

Oh, excuse me. I just noticed your spelling. You didn't say Mr. Wright, you said Mr. Right. I apologize. So sorry. My mistake.

The change in spelling gives your question a whole new dimension. And some added problems. Just as finding Mr. Wright is fairly easy, finding Mr. Right is fairly difficult. This is true whether you are looking for Mr. Right or Miss Right. (I suggest women look for Mr. Right and men look for Miss Right. In my experience, this is usually the most productive and fulfilling.)

Finding Mr. or Miss Right is important. What makes finding Mr. or Miss Right so important is that many of us know what it was like to have found Mr. or Miss Wrong. Even though he or she seemed Right.

Just think back to the beginning of the relationship. When you first met him or her, she or he looked like Mr. or Miss Right. You thought there was a good chance he was, didn't you? Of course, you did. Otherwise you wouldn't have started going out with him. Dating him. Going steady with him. Dreaming of a future with him.

Then something happened. It turned out he wasn't so right after all.

You usually discover he or she isn't the right one when your relationship begins to turn into something you dread rather than love. You'd rather be anywhere than with him. Her laugh used to sound wonderfully cute. Now it sounds like a cackle—"I'll bet a house fell on her sister," you say to yourself. His sense of humor, which once seemed so fresh and offbeat, now seems childish, immature, and just plain stupid. You find out he's moody. She is way too serious. You criticize him. She destroys you. You can't seem to do anything right in her eyes, and she bugs you to death. It becomes a lot more like war and less like peace.

This is very difficult. You see your dream relationship beginning to crumble. You don't know what to do. Sometimes you stick it out with someone who is making your life miserable and whose life you're turning into hell, just because you don't know what else to do. You've become accustomed to always being with that person. You both have turned out to be someone different from who you thought the other was. And nobody wants to hurt anybody else, or be the bad guy, so you just keep on, all the while wishing you had the guts to leave. Your love for that person has turned. It probably hasn't turned to hate. It's not that. But you know you'd be better off alone. This isn't Mr. or Miss Right.

For you, that is. That's not to say this person won't be Mr. or Miss Right for somebody else. It doesn't even mean he or she isn't a nice or good person, even wonderful—just with someone else.

Sometimes you know that right away. Other times it takes a little longer. Still other times it takes a lot longer. If it has taken a while to get out of that relationship, you promise yourself to be a lot more careful in the future. The next time you want to find the *real* Mr. or Miss Right. Not someone who looks like he or she might be.

We have all been there. We all want to find that special person who will be right for us. So we search high and low. We spend hours fantasizing what he or she will look and be like. What our life together will be like. We make Mr. or Miss Right almost a god or goddess, an ideal that will never be real.

Maybe we try too hard. Maybe Mr. or Miss Right is already in our life. Mine was.

When I first met Nancy, I didn't dream I'd ever marry her. I wasn't planning on marrying anyone. But here I am now married to her and I can't imagine my life without her. I love her and am glad I married her. But when I first saw her, marriage was not on my mind.

Nancy and I got to be friends. Over the years we found that we liked a lot of the same things. We have a similar (if warped) sense of humor. The same ideals are important to us—ideals like family, holidays, faith, and helping others. We shared a lot of the same friends. We had a lot of things in common. And we really liked each other.

That's not to say there aren't differences. I am a city boy from Ohio and she is a farm girl from Indiana. I went to college (actually colleges) and she didn't. She was a straight-*A* student and I was . . . well, never mind. We aren't even the same age. She likes a lot of country-western music and I love rock and roll. I play sports and she watches sports.

What makes her Miss Right for me is the simple fact that I like her. I really like her. I respect her, I value her, I love her with my whole heart, but most of all I like her. She is my best friend. We don't always agree. I do lots of things differently from the way she would. I think she gets way too involved in projects and other stuff. Yet through it all I have no doubt that she is my Miss Right. And she believes I am her Mr. Right.

Why?

Because it feels right. When I am with her, there is a peace about my life. She brings out the best in me. She enables me to be the person I should be. And I do the same for her.

How do you find Mr. or Miss Right? Start by looking at your friends. Who among them do you like the best? Could he or she be Mr. or Miss Right? Could be. Don't overlook the obvious. Prince Charming is just as likely to be driving an old Escort as riding around on a white charger. Look at who you most enjoy being with.

That's not to say finding Mr. or Miss Right will be easy. It won't. But there is another place you can turn. To God.

Don't be afraid to ask God for some help in this. God wants us to be in the best relationships—not the worst.

Ask God to help you find the person that's right for you. Don't ask at 11:00 and expect him to knock on your door at 11:15. That won't happen. Don't make it so hard, either. Don't rush it. Relax and enjoy life. Take all the time you need. Experience all of life you can. Besides, Mr. Right might be that guy sitting in front of the house right now, waiting to take you and the rest of the gang for pizza.

Or you may not have even met him yet.

So relax. Kick back and enjoy. There is one Mr. Right you can have in your life right now if you'll just ask. That's God. And He was there all the time.